A New Life Awaits!

ADDICTED

TO

Grace

*The only addiction that
can set you free!*

Brad Robertson

Addicted To Grace

A New Life Awaits!

Addicted To Grace
Copyright ©2019 by Brad Robertson

First Edition - 2019

ISBN   978-0-578-40776-0

The names of people mentioned in this book have been changed. However, the content of Brad's encounters with each of them is true.

5th Printing

DEDICATION

I dedicate this book to those who are suffering from addictions and to their families. I know your pain is great. I pray you discover the riches of God's grace that can heal your pain and lead you to a new life.

TABLE OF CONTENTS

PART ONE | A CLOSER LOOK AT GRACE

PART TWO | A CLOSER LOOK AT ADDICTION

PART ONE
A Closer Look At Grace

1

God Is Reaching Out To You With Grace

All this is for your benefit, so that the grace of God that is reaching more and more people will result in thanksgiving overflowing to God.
2 Corinthians 4:15

PEOPLE DON'T START OUT IN LIFE dreaming of being addicted to something and then experiencing the destruction of their addiction. Rather, they start out in life dreaming of being someone and experiencing the joy of seeing their dreams become reality. But somewhere along the way, the addiction begins. Then, slowly and sadly, the addiction takes complete control of their lives, bringing utter ruin and destruction, causing them to lose everything. Where they once spent their days dreaming of what they would become, they now spend their days in shame, guilt, and condemnation, dreaming of what could have been.

How do people filled with such hope for the future, dreaming of what they would one day become, end up hurting themselves and the ones they love, living in misery and pain, and dreaming only of what could have been?

You Started Out With Hope
Maybe this is you. You can relate. You started your life with such hope for your future. You dreamed of what you would one day become. But now your days are spent in bondage to your addiction. You live your days in misery, pain, guilt, shame, condemnation, and regret. You hate yourself for what you have done, for what you have become. You find it impossible to forgive yourself. Your shame, guilt, and pain is so great suicide has possibly become an option.

In addition to all of these feelings, you feel distant from God. You made promises to God to do better. You promised him you would stop drinking, stop using drugs, stop looking at pornography, stop gambling, stop buying, or stop doing what you do and going where you go. You promised him you would become a better person, son, daughter, husband, wife, father, or mother. You were sincere in making these promises, but as sincere as you were, you failed. Again and again, you failed.

Not only are you angry and disappointed with yourself, but you feel God is angry and disappointed, too. You feel you can never be close to God because you have done too much, gone too far, and broken too many promises. You are not alone. Many people feel this way. This is how Ted felt.

Thanks For Teaching Me About Grace!
Ted, who suffered with addiction, walked into my office and said, "I thought I could never be close to God again. But because of grace, I realize I can be close to God. Thank you so much for teaching me about grace!"

Ted became addicted to grace!

Teaching people about grace is what this book is about. It is about being under the influence of grace. It is about being intoxicated with grace. It is about being addicted to grace!

God Is Reaching Out To You
God is the God of grace. He is full of love for you. He is not angry or disappointed with you. He is the God who reaches out to you in your disgust. He is the God who reaches out to you in your despair. He is the God who reaches out to you in your darkness. He is the God who reaches out to you in your sin. The God you thought hated you loves you. He is reaching out to you with grace. He is reaching out to you with love, compassion, kindness, and forgiveness. He longs to restore you through his grace. He is reaching out to you now.

Wherever your addiction has led you, God's grace finds you. Titus 2:11 says, *"For the grace of God has appeared that offers salvation to all people."* No matter who you are...no matter what you have done...no matter where you are...God is offering you his grace. He is reaching out to you with grace. Receive his grace.

Ted received God's grace, and it changed his life. Grace will change your life too! Just like Ted, you do not have to live another day in pain, misery, shame, guilt, condemnation, or regret. Instead, you can begin living in the peace, joy, and freedom of grace. Through God's grace, you will even be empowered to dream again.

Because of God's grace, a new life awaits!

2

God Is Reaching Out To You With Love

So God created mankind in his own image, in the image of God he created them; male and female he created them.
Genesis 1:27

YOU WERE CREATED BY GOD to be loved by him and to experience a life of joy, peace, and fulfillment. You were not created by God to be controlled by an addiction. You were not created by God to be destroyed by an addiction. You were not created by God to lose your family, your job, your friends, your peace, your dreams, and possibly even your life through an addiction.

Created To Experience And Express God's Love

You were created by God in his very image. The image of God is love. The Bible says love comes from God (1 John 4:7) and God is love (1 John 4:9). You were created to experience God's love and express his love to others.

Through experiencing and expressing God's love, you will become a whole, healthy person, built up with God's love and building up others as his love flows through you. This is how God created all mankind, in his image, with a built-in need to be loved by him and a built-in need to love others.

But something happened.

Walking Away From God's Love

Mankind walked away from God's love, and in doing so, chose to live independently from God. By walking away from God, we separated ourselves from life's very source, the love of God. Everything we needed to be complete, to function for the purpose we were created, was in the love of God for us, his love in us, and his love flowing through us. Yet we walked away from his love, our very source of life.

I wrote about our walking away from God's love in my book, *The Story of Grace*. I compared mankind's decision to live independently from God to a fish choosing to live independently from the water. Everything the fish needs is in the water. Its very source of life is the water. It is the water that brings the fish to life and provides what the fish needs to live. Separated from the water, the fish dies. Separated from God, mankind dies.

All that God created was good. One of his creations was a beautiful garden for mankind to enjoy called the Garden of Eden. In love, God told Adam, the first man, that he could eat from any tree in the garden, but if he ate from the tree of the knowledge of good and evil, he would die (Genesis 2:15-17). Soon, Adam ate from the tree, and death entered the human race, spreading to everyone (Romans 5:12).

The Serpent's Lies
Genesis 3:1-5 explains how this happened. The serpent strategically approached Eve, having the following conversation with her:

> *"Did God really say, 'You must not eat from any tree in the garden'?" The woman said to the serpent, "We may eat fruit from the trees in the garden, but God did say, 'You must not eat fruit from the tree that is in the middle of the garden, and you must not touch it, or you will die.'" "You will not certainly die," the serpent said to the woman. "For God knows that when you eat from it your eyes will be opened, and you will be like God, knowing good and evil."*

God Isn't Loving Or Good
Notice what the serpent, who is Satan, is strategically doing in

these verses. He is casting seeds of doubt into the heart and mind of Eve about the loving nature and goodness of God. He is seeking to distort the image of God by attempting to convince her God is not good or loving but is unloving and is withholding good from her by not allowing her to eat the fruit from the tree of the knowledge of good and evil.

Satan knew if he could distort the loving image of God in the heart and mind of Eve by casting seeds of doubt about his goodness and love, then he could eventually persuade her to disobey God's instructions concerning the tree, ultimately bringing destruction and death into her life.

We see the result of Satan's strategy in the following verses:

> *When the woman saw that the fruit of the tree was good for food and pleasing to the eye, and desirable for gaining wisdom, she took some and ate it. She also gave some to her husband, who was with her, and he ate it. Then the eyes of both of them were opened, and they realized they were naked; so they sewed fig leaves together and made coverings for themselves* (Genesis 3:6-7).

Satan's strategy worked. He successfully convinced Eve, through his lies, that God was not a loving God and he was withholding good from her and Adam by not allowing them to eat from the tree of the knowledge of good and evil. Once she was convinced God was not loving or good, she ate the fruit of the tree. Adam, too, ate of the tree; yet he was not deceived. His act of eating from the tree was disobedience to God's loving warning to not eat from the tree.

Suddenly, their eyes were opened to good and evil. They now possessed the capacity to do evil. Through this one act of disobedience, inspired by the satanic lies that God is not loving or good, the evil destruction of sin and death entered the human race. In the heart of mankind, sin replaced love.

Also entering the heart of mankind was guilt, shame, condemnation, regret, and fear. The following verses in Genesis 3:8-10 provide evidence of this:

> *Then the eyes of both of them were opened, and they realized they were naked; so they sewed fig leaves together and made coverings for themselves. Then the man and his wife heard the Lord God as he was walking in the garden in the cool of the day, and they hid from the Lord God among the trees of the garden. But the Lord God called to the man, "Where are you?" He answered, "I heard you in the garden, and I was afraid because I was naked; so I hid."*

The heart of mankind, once containing the love of God, now contained sin and its consequences: guilt, shame, condemnation, regret, and fear. The loving relationship they previously enjoyed with God was severed.

Regret began to set into the heart and mind of Adam and Eve. They hated what they did. They hated who they became. If only they could go back and undo it all.

We all know how this feels.

Still Loved By God

The decision Adam and Eve made did not change how God felt toward them. He still loved them...unconditionally. His nature was still love. His image was still love. Nothing they could do or had done would cause God not to love them. And it was this love God had for them that would ultimately heal their heart and mind.

God Calls Out To Adam And Eve

This love is expressed by God in what he did after Adam and Eve walked away from his love. Having been persuaded by

Satan that God was not good or loving, Adam and Eve hid from God, afraid of his rejection and punishment. But God, in love, came to Adam and Eve. He called out to Adam, asking, "Where are you?" God did not ask Adam where he was because he could not find him. God was not looking for Adam. He knew where Adam was. He asked Adam this question because Adam needed to admit where he was for Eve and himself to experiencing healing.

By bringing their guilt, shame, condemnation, and regret into the light of his love, healing would begin. But as long as they hid from God in fear of his rejection and punishment, their pain and misery would persist. They would descend further and further into the darkness of their despair.

Adam And Eve Become Consumed With Self
Adam And Eve Hid From Each Other
Not only did Adam and Eve hide from God, but they also hid from each other because they had become self-conscious. They became totally focused upon themselves. The fear of rejection entered their hearts. Craving each other's acceptance, but fearing each other's rejection, they hid from one another by clothing themselves in fig leaves. They attempted to cover externally the guilt and shame they felt internally.

Adam And Eve Judged Each Other
Now, being consumed with themselves and fearing the other's rejection, they no longer felt loved by one another, and they could no longer show love to one another. So rather than loving one another, which they were created to do, they began to judge one another.

> *And he said, "Who told you that you were naked? Have you eaten from the tree that I commanded you not to eat from?" The man said, "The woman you put here with me—she gave me some fruit from the tree, and I ate it."*

Then the Lord God said to the woman, "What is this you have done?" The woman said, "The serpent deceived me, and I ate." (Genesis 3:11-13)

Adam And Eve Refused To Accept Responsibility

A careful reading of these verses reveals the judgment of Adam toward Eve. Immediately, coming across angry at Eve, Adam judges her as the one who is at fault, denying his own role in eating of the tree and blaming Eve for his failure. Not only does Adam judge Eve as the guilty one, but he angrily blames God as the one who is ultimately responsible for his choice. By this response to God, Adam demonstrates he no longer sees God as good. He now views God as the one who created the problem. Eve, like Adam, denies her responsibility in eating of the tree. Refusing to accept responsibility, she blames the serpent.

So we see that after Adam and Eve chose to walk away from God's love, their hearts were no longer controlled by love but by judgment. This judgment is displayed in their response of denial, anger, and blame.

The Promised Child

Yet God never stopped loving and being good to Adam and Eve. He made a promise that a woman from the human race would give birth to a male child, and this male child will crush the head of the serpent (Genesis 3:15). This child would be proof of God's goodness and love. This child would be proof of his grace.

The Promised Child Would Prove God Is Loving And Good

The venom of a serpent is in its head. The devil, Satan, had injected his poisonous lies into the heart and mind of Adam and Eve, convincing them God wasn't loving or good. Yet this coming child would crush the head of Satan, delivering a death blow to this liar, proving to all, no matter how great our sin, his love is greater. His grace is greater!

The first picture of grace we see in the Bible is Genesis 3:21

when God clothed Adam and Eve in animal skins.

> *The Lord God made garments of skin for Adam and his wife and clothed them.*

Remember, God lovingly warned Adam that if he ate of the tree he would die. Spiritually, he died, meaning his relationship with God was severed. I would compare this spiritual death to a light being separated from its power source. Without the power source, the light dies. Without the love of God within Adam, Adam died. This spiritual death spread to all men (Romans 5:12). We are all born spiritually dead (Ephesians 2:1).

Yet God's heart was to be reconciled to people and for his Spirit to live in and pour his love into our hearts. He created us to be in a love relationship with him and for our hearts to contain his love. Through God's grace in Jesus, God reconciled us to himself, making it possible for people to be reconciled to him (2 Corinthians 5:18-6:2) and for his Spirit to live in and pour his love into our hearts (Romans 5:5).

Not only did Adam die spiritually when he sinned, but also, through his sin, physical death entered the entire human race. Notice, Adam and Eve did not die an immediate physical death when they sinned. Instead, God in grace, provided an innocent animal to die in their place. This animal, serving as a substitute for Adam and Eve's sin, may have possibly been a lamb, symbolizing Jesus, the Lamb of God, would come and die for the sins of all people.

> *The next day John saw Jesus coming toward him and said, "Look, the Lamb of God, who takes away the sin of the world!"* (John 1:29)

The Promised Child Would Die For Everyone

The Bible looks forward to the One God promised would come and deliver the ultimate death blow to Satan, crushing his head and exposing his lies.

The letter of Hebrews describes the coming of this Promised One, Jesus, as being fully God (Hebrews 1) and fully man (Hebrews 2). By grace, Jesus would taste death for everyone, freeing us all from the power of Satan and the fearful grip of death he had on us.

> *But we do see Jesus, who was made lower than the angels for a little while, now crowned with glory and honor because he suffered death, so that by the grace of God he might taste death for everyone...Since the children have flesh and blood, he too shared in their humanity so that by his death he might break the power of him who holds the power of death—that is, the devil— and free those who all their lives were held in slavery by their fear of death.* (Hebrews 2:9, 14-15)

Satan's goal is to keep people in the fearful grip of his lies by convincing them God isn't good or loving. But through the grace God has given us in Jesus, he has revealed to us he really is good and loving, and he is reaching out to us with grace.

3

God Is Reaching Out To You With Forgiveness

All this is from God, who reconciled us to himself through Christ and gave us the ministry of reconciliation: that God was reconciling the world to himself in Christ, not counting people's sins against them.
2 Corinthians 5:18-19

SATAN ATTEMPTS TO POISON your heart and mind with his venomous lies that God isn't good and doesn't love you. He tries to convince you that God is angry with you and has rejected you because of your addiction...because of your sin. Yet, no matter how bad your addiction and how great your sin, his love is greater!

God Demonstrates His Love
The proof of God's love is in Jesus, the male child whom he promised would come. Jesus, in John 3:16, says God loved the people of the world so deeply that he was moved to send his Son into our darkness and despair, so that anyone who believed in him would not die but live forever in God's eternal kingdom.

The Death Of Jesus Reveals How Much God Loves You!
God's love for us is demonstrated by Jesus dying for the sins of the entire human race. Romans 5:8 says, *"God demonstrates his love for us in this: while we were yet sinners, Christ died for us."* The death of Jesus reveals just how much God loves us...just how much he loves you!

> *This is how God showed his love among us: He sent his one and only Son into the world that we might live through him. This is love: not that we loved God, but that he loved us and sent his Son as an atoning sacrifice for our sins.* (1 John 4:9-10)

God's Not Mad At You!

God's not mad at you. He is not out to punish you. He loves you. It is through his love for you, demonstrated in Jesus, that you can live. Satan, through the addiction, is seeking to take your life. Yet God has not stopped loving you. He is reaching out to you in love to give you life.

God reaching out to the human race in love, reaching out to you in love, is called grace. In the previous chapter, we read Hebrews 2:9 which says, *"But we do see Jesus who was made lower than the angels for a little while, now crowned with glory and honor because he suffered death, so that by the grace of God he might taste death for everyone."*

God Knew You Would Need Grace

God knew before time began that we would all sin and be in desperate need of his grace. That is why he gave us grace in Jesus before time began.

> *This grace was given us in Christ Jesus before the beginning of time, but it has now been revealed through the appearing of our Savior, Christ Jesus...* (2 Timothy 2:9)

Think about what this means.

God knew about your addiction before you were ever born. He knew the things you would do. He knew the places you would go. He knew the promises you would break. He knew the people you would hurt. He knew you would need grace. He knew you would need forgiveness. So, because of his great love for you, he provided grace for your forgiveness. He is not mad at you. He loves you. He is not counting your sins against you. Your sins, along with the sins of the world, were counted against Jesus...all of them!

> *All this is from God, who reconciled us to himself through*

Christ and gave us the ministry of reconciliation: that God was reconciling the world to himself in Christ, not counting people's sins against them.
(2 Corinthians 5:18-19)

God is reaching out to you with his forgiveness. He is not waiting on you to ask him to forgive you, he has already forgiven you! He is patiently waiting on you to accept by faith the forgiveness he has fully and forever provided for you in Jesus.

The Good News God Wants Me To Tell You!

This is the good news I have the privilege and honor of sharing with you. As God's ambassador of grace, he wants me to tell you he is not mad at you. He wants me to tell you he is not angry with you. He wants me to tell you he is not condemning of you. He wants me to tell you he is not frustrated with you. He wants me to tell you he is not out to punish you. As his ambassador, he wants me to tell you the penalty for your sin was paid for by Jesus. He wants me to tell you he loves you and is not counting your sins against you.

How do I know God wants me to tell you this as his ambassador of the good news of grace? Take a look at the following verses in 1 Corinthians 5:18-6:2:

All this is from God, who reconciled us to himself through Christ and gave us the ministry of reconciliation: that God was reconciling the world to himself in Christ, not counting people's sins against them. And he has committed to us the message of reconciliation. We are therefore Christ's ambassadors, as though God were making his appeal through us. We implore you on Christ's behalf: Be reconciled to God. God made him who had no sin to be sin for us, so that in him we might become the righteousness of God. As God's co-workers we urge you not to receive God's grace in vain. For he says, "In the time of my favor I heard you, and in the day of salvation

*I helped you." I tell you, now is the time of God's favor,
now is the day of salvation.*

Good News...God's Not Counting Your Sins Against You!

This is the good news of grace! Do you see it? God is not counting your sins against you. Why not? Because all your sins were counted against Jesus. If all your sins were counted against Jesus, then how many are left to be counted against you? None! Jesus became sin for you, for the world, for us all, that we may become righteous in God's sight by faith (Romans 3:21-25).

Good News...God Hears You And Wants To Help You!

2 Corinthians 6:2 says God hears you and wants to help you. He has heard your cries of pain. He has heard your cries for help. Today is the day of God's favor. Today is the day of God's kindness. Today is the day of God's grace. Today, right now, God is reaching out to you with grace, meaning he is reaching out to you with kindness and forgiveness. Accept his forgiveness.

Accept God's Forgiveness

And how do you accept his forgiveness? You accept his forgiveness by believing in Jesus.

> *"Therefore, my friends, I want you to know that through Jesus the forgiveness of sins is proclaimed to you. Through him everyone who believes is set free from every sin..."* (Acts 13:38-39)

By believing Jesus died for all your sins is how to accept God's forgiveness for every sin. When you believe, you receive all of God's forgiveness for all your sins for all time. Colossians 2:13-14 says, *"...God made you alive with Christ. He forgave us all our sins..."*

The letter of Hebrews says that at one time, for all sin, and for all people Jesus offered himself.

He sacrificed for their sins once for all when he offered himself. (Hebrews 7:27)

But he has appeared once for all at the culmination of the ages to do away with sin by the sacrifice of himself. (Hebrews 9:26)

But when [Jesus] had offered for all time one sacrifice for sins, he sat down at the right hand of God. (Hebrews 10:12)

Good News...God Remembers Your Sins No More!

Now that Jesus, through his one-time payment for all people and for all sin, has shed his blood for the forgiveness of our sins, God remembers our sins no more. He remembers your sins no more. Hebrews 10:17-18 says,

"Their sins and lawless acts I will remember no more. And where these have been forgiven, sacrifice for sin is no longer necessary."

Love Replaces Fear

Once people experience the revelation of God's love and forgiveness in their hearts and minds, fear will leave. They will no longer live in fear of condemnation because they now understand Jesus was condemned for all their sins. There is no condemnation for sins left (Romans 8:1). They have been made perfect in love because they know love paid the penalty for all their sins, and they have been forgiven of all their sins (1 John 4:9-10, 18).

When love comes into a person's heart, fear leaves. When fear leaves, peace and joy come.

The Joy And Peace Of Forgiveness

Look at the following verses about the peace and joy a person experiences who realizes he is forgiven.

"Blessed are those whose transgressions are forgiven, whose sins are covered. Blessed is the one whose sin the Lord will never count against them."
(Romans 4:7-8)

The word "blessed" in this verse means a person is delighted, or overflowing with great peace and joy, because God will never judge this person for his sins. All his sins were forever paid for by Jesus. As a result, God will never count this person's sins against him.

"Forgiven" means God has freely and fully given forgiveness to a person. He will never count this person's sins against him or her. God is not keeping a record of this person's sins because he remembers them no more. This forgiveness has come through Jesus and is received by believing in Jesus.

God's Forgiveness Is For You!

You may think God's forgiveness is for others but not for you. You may have the thought your sins are far too many and far worse than others. However, Romans 4:7-8 is a quotation from Psalm 32:1-2 following King David's experience of God's forgiveness after coveting Uriah's wife, Bathsheba, having an adulterous affair with her, arranging for Uriah to be murdered, and then covering it up by lying about it all.

Just like King David's sins were not too many or too bad, neither are yours. Dwell on the truth of God's forgiveness toward you. Dwell on the truth that Jesus paid for all your sins for all time and God will never count your sins against you. Dwell on the truth that God remembers your sins no more. Now delight in these truths for a lifetime! Let the fullness of God's forgiveness flow into your heart, and let the joy of knowing you are forgiven bring peace to your heart. Your sins have been fully and forever paid for by Jesus. God will never count your sins against you. You are blessed!

I Just Can't Forgive Myself

Once, after speaking on forgiveness, someone approached me and said, "I believe God has forgiven me, but I just can't forgive myself. How do I forgive myself?"

This is a good question. Possibly, you are asking the same question. You believe God has forgiven you, but you are having trouble forgiving yourself.

Because God will never count your sins against you, since they were fully and forever counted against Jesus, you no longer have to count your sins against yourself. You have been beating yourself up long enough because of your sins. You have been beating yourself up long enough because of your past failures. You have been beating yourself up long enough because of your addiction. Because you continue to beat yourself up, you remain in your addiction. Your regret, guilt, shame, and condemnation continue to fuel your addiction. Today, stop beating yourself up, set yourself free from Satan's grip of guilt and start believing God has forgiven you, fully and forever. Then, with the same faith, the same belief, forgive yourself. King David did. You can too.

Tell Yourself You Are Forgiven

By faith, tell yourself every day God has fully and forever forgiven you of all your sins. By faith, tell yourself every day that because God has fully and forever forgiven you of all your sins, you choose to forgive yourself fully and forever of all your sins.

The act of experiencing God's forgiveness and then passing it to yourself is done by faith. It has to be by faith, because your feelings will tell you that God hasn't forgiven you. Your feelings will tell you that you are terrible person. Your feelings will tell you that you don't deserve to be forgiven. Your feelings will tell you that you should pay for your own sins.

Also, Satan will come along and confirm what your feelings are telling you. He will seek to get you to agree with your feelings. At this point, in direct opposition to your feelings and to the lies Satan is telling you, tell yourself that God has forgiven you and that you have forgiven yourself. Refuse to believe Satan's lies that keep you in bondage.

Tyler Told Himself He Was Forgiven

One day, as I was having a conversation with Tyler about his addiction, he told me he did not deserve God's forgiveness, nor deserve to forgive himself. He believed he would have to live with guilt for the rest of his life.

Tyler was so ashamed of what he did that he could not tell me about it during our counseling sessions. I told him about receiving God's forgiveness and forgiving himself. I encouraged Tyler to daily, by faith, in total contrast to his feelings, believe God had forgiven him, and, with that same faith, forgive himself. Tyler began to do daily what I had told him.

One day, I looked at Tyler and he had a big smile on his face. I knew the reason for his smile. Tyler had begun to daily, by faith, choose to believe God had forgiven him and to extend forgiveness to himself. As he daily embraced the truth that God had forgiven him, and then by faith, forgave himself, joy and peace began to flow into his heart and show up on his face. Tyler became addicted to grace!

The same is true for you. Today, in total contrast to how you feel, by faith, choose to believe God has forgiven you and is not counting your sins against you, and then extend forgiveness to yourself. Tell yourself every day the following:

God has forgiven me. I forgive myself.

As you do this, over the course of time, you will experience the blessing of forgiveness. The burden of guilt will be replaced by the blessing of grace. Peace and joy will enter your heart. A big smile will appear on your face. Then, like Tyler, you will become addicted to grace. And I have discovered those who become addicted to grace make great ambassadors of grace!

4

God Reached Out To Paul With Grace

The grace of our Lord was poured out on me abundantly,
along with the faith and love that are in Christ Jesus.
1 Timothy 1:14

IF THERE EVER WAS ANYONE who was addicted to grace, it was Paul. He became one of the greatest ambassadors of grace this world has ever known. You may be familiar with him.

Paul, at one time, was a religious terrorist. He was responsible for the deaths of many people. He was responsible for tearing families apart. However, one day, while on one of his religious rampages of terror, the ascended Jesus reached out to Paul in grace, pouring his grace upon him. This abundant outpouring of grace totally changed Paul's life. Paul tells about this outpouring of grace by saying:

> *Even though I was once a blasphemer and a persecutor and a violent man, I was shown mercy because I acted in ignorance and unbelief. The grace of our Lord was poured out on me abundantly, along with the faith and love that are in Christ Jesus. Here is a trustworthy saying that deserves full acceptance: Christ Jesus came into the world to save sinners—of whom I am the worst. But for that very reason I was shown mercy so that in me, the worst of sinners, Christ Jesus might display his immense patience as an example for those who would believe in him and receive eternal life. Now to the King eternal, immortal, invisible, the only God, be honor and glory for ever and ever. Amen.* (1 Timothy 1:13-17)

Paul Is An Example Of A Person Changed By Grace
As you can see by reading Paul's own words, grace changed his

life. He began seeing himself as a person on whom God's grace was poured out abundantly. He realized his very life served as an example of the unlimited grace of God that is available for all people. Paul is your example, my example, and the world's example that God's grace is available for all, with no exceptions!

Paul Became Addicted To Grace

Through this encounter with Jesus, when he poured grace upon Paul abundantly, Paul became addicted to grace. Grace totally changed his life. Grace encouraged him. Grace empowered him. Grace energized him. Grace emancipated him. His whole life became characterized by grace. As this verse indicates, his whole life became controlled by grace.

> *But by the grace of God I am what I am, and his grace to me was not without effect. No, I worked harder than all of them--yet not I, but the grace of God that was with me.* (1 Corinthians 15:10)

From this verse, we see that grace took total control of Paul's life. Isn't this what an addiction does, it totally takes control of our lives? The addiction controls everything about us. It controls what we do. It controls where we go. It controls how we act. Our lives begin to be characterized and controlled by the addiction.

Our Lives Become Addicted To Grace

Becoming addicted to grace operates in the same way. Our lives begin to be controlled and characterized by grace. What we do, where we go, and how we begin to be influenced by grace. We become addicted to grace.

Paul, teaching on the powerful impact of grace upon our lives says,

> *For the grace of God has appeared that offers salvation to all people. It teaches us to say "No" to ungodliness and*

worldly passions, and to live self-controlled, upright and godly lives in this present age, while we wait for the blessed hope—the appearing of the glory of our great God and Savior, Jesus Christ, who gave himself for us to redeem us from all wickedness and to purify for himself a people that are his very own, eager to do what is good. (Titus 2:11-14)

There are many believers, along with Bible teachers and pastors, who underestimate the power of grace. They criticize grace teachers of teaching "cheap grace," "greasy grace," or "easy believism." They accuse us of "being light on sin" and "giving people a license to sin." They believe grace causes people to sin more. As a result, they seek to suppress the teaching of the good news of God's grace. This happened to me while serving as a counselor/teacher at a Christian addiction recovery ministry.

What You Are Teaching Will Cause People To Sin More
For a year and a half, while at the recovery center, I taught from the letters of Romans, Galatians, Ephesians, Philippians, Colossians, and Hebrews. In addition, I taught those in my classes about the old covenant of law and the new covenant of grace, as well as the full, final, forever, and finished work of Jesus. It was obvious the truth of grace was changing the lives of many men.

This life-change was evident when men at the graduation ceremony of the addiction recovery center consistently thanked me publicly for teaching them about grace. Over and over again, many of the men would tell those attending the graduation ceremony that the teaching of grace changed their lives.

While at this Christian recovery ministry, I soon discovered that many believers, as well as many Bible teachers and pastors, are hostile to grace. I began to experience daily their rejection and criticism. It soon became apparent to me why I was experiencing such hostility.

One day, a staff member who worked at the recovery

ministry came into my office and told me I needed to stop teaching so much about grace. I asked him why. He said because the recovery ministry would lose its reputation with churches and pastors. Then, consequently, they would lose financial support, as well as recommendations for those in their churches to participate in the recovery and addiction program. He also said, teaching grace would cause the men to sin more and return to their addiction.

At this point, I attempted to explain from the Bible the truth of grace and how through grace the ministry would receive more financial support and impact many more men, but he did not want to hear it.

An Under Appreciation Of Grace

Sadly, some believers, Bible teachers, and pastors under appreciate grace because they have an over appreciation of themselves, believing they are not as sinful as others. Because of this elevated view of themselves, resulting in bragging about their morality and religious activity, they are unaware of their total need for grace. Therefore, they have a limited appreciation for grace.

Since they have a limited appreciation for grace, they have no understanding of the power of grace to change lives. Instead, they slander the grace of God by referring to it as "cheap grace," "greasy grace," and "easy believism." And in doing so, they slander God himself.

An example of this elevated view of oneself was displayed in a Bible teacher and Pastor I once knew. He would often brag to his congregation that he did not sin. He was serious in saying this. If he did sin, he said it would be only for something like overeating. Consequently, this teacher was unable to appreciate grace because he did not see his need for grace.

Well, it wasn't long until I was called into the Associate Executive Director's office at the recovery center. He brought me into his office and told me I was being released from my position because what I was teaching and what the recovery ministry believed were not the same. My response was that if they did not believe the letters of Romans, Galatians, Ephesians, Philippians, Colossians, and Hebrews, and if they did not believe in the new covenant and the full, final, forever, and finished work of Jesus, then yes, we believed differently. I gently tried to explain the gospel of grace to him, but, in his visible anger toward me, he refused to listen.

It is sad how some believers, Bible teachers, and pastors, who are saved by grace, reject the very grace that saved them. This is what is so amazing about Paul. At one time, he was one of these people. He was a teacher of the Scriptures. Yet when he experienced the abundant outpouring of grace upon his life, his life was completely changed.

God Calls Paul To Tell People All Over The World About Grace
Following Paul's experience with grace, God called him to be the very one who would make grace known to people all over the world. This calling of God upon Paul's life started the moment he was conceived in his mother's womb.

> *...God, who set me apart from my mother's womb and called me by his grace, was pleased to reveal his Son in me so that I might preach him among the Gentiles...* (Galatians 1:15)

Paul is an example that no matter how great our sin, God's grace is greater. Our sin cannot separate us from God's calling upon our lives.

Maybe you have felt your sins have separated you from what God has called you to do. I have good news for you...no great news for you! Your sins have not separated you from what God has called you to do. God is reaching out to you now with grace, just as Jesus reached out to Paul. God still wants to use you to do great things, empowered and energized by his grace.

After his grace-encounter with Jesus, Paul was given the assignment of sharing the good news of God's grace.

> *However, I consider my life worth nothing to me; my only*
> *aim is to finish the race and complete the task the Lord*
> *Jesus has given me—the task of testifying to the good*
> *news of God's grace.* (Acts 20:24)

Nothing Was More Important
Nothing in his life was more important to Paul than telling people about the good news of God's grace. Because his life had been so impacted by grace, he was compelled to take grace around the globe!

During his life, he shared with thousands of people the message of grace Jesus had given him. This message was that God was not counting people's sins against them but wanted a relationship with them. He traveled all over the Roman Empire to share this message. In doing so, he started churches in many of the cities he visited.

Paul Endured Hardships So Others Could Hear About Grace
Because Paul was addicted to grace, and because he was an ambassador of grace, on assignment from Jesus himself, and because he had such a passion for people to hear about grace, he would do anything to reach more and more people with the good news of God's grace, even if he had to endure tremendous hardships and sufferings.

Paul writes in 2 Corinthians 4:7-16 about the hardships and sufferings he experienced and why he was willing to endure such difficulties, never giving up on getting God's grace to people.

> *But we have this treasure* [the good news of God's grace]
> *in jars of clay to show that this all-surpassing power is*
> *from God and not from us. We are hard pressed on every*

side, but not crushed; perplexed, but not in despair; persecuted, but not abandoned; struck down, but not destroyed. We always carry around in our body the death of Jesus, so that the life of Jesus may also be revealed in our body. For we who are alive are always being given over to death for Jesus' sake, so that his life may also be revealed in our mortal body. So then, death is at work in us, but life is at work in you. All this is for your benefit, so that the grace that is reaching more and more people may cause thanksgiving to overflow to the glory of God. Therefore, we do not lose heart.

No matter how difficult the hardship, no matter how painful the suffering, Paul never gave up in getting grace to people. Because he was willing to die to deliver grace to people, many lives were changed. As a result of these life-changing encounters with grace, gratitude overflowed from their hearts to God.

After The Cross, The Word Grace Is Used Over 150 Times

Before Jesus died on the cross, the word grace (in the Greek language the word for grace is *charis*) was used about 7 times in the books of Matthew, Mark, Luke, and John. Following the death of Jesus, the word grace is used over 150 times in the Bible. The majority of these times are written by Paul. Talk about addicted to grace!

Through Paul's experience of grace, he went on to write the majority of the New Testament. His writings capture his passion for grace and what grace produced in his life and in the lives of others. His writings continue to change the lives of people today.

Your Life Is Not Over!

Because of grace, your life is not over. Like Paul, God will use you to do great things. His grace will become an encouraging, energizing, and empowering force in your life. Your life will serve as an example to many people of the power of his grace to change lives. Because of God's grace working so powerfully in you and reaching more and more people through you, people will see how great God is, and they will see the greatness of his grace. As a result, their lives will be changed, and they, too, will become addicted to grace!

5

God Wants You To Understand His Grace

We always thank God, the Father of our Lord Jesus Christ,
when we pray for you, because we have heard of your faith in
Christ Jesus and of the love you have for all God's people —
the faith and love that spring from the hope stored up for you
in heaven and about which you have already heard in the true
message of the gospel that has come to you. In the same way,
the gospel is bearing fruit and growing throughout the whole
world—just as it has been doing among you since
the day you heard it and understood God's
grace in all its truth.
Colossians 1:3-6

WHEN PEOPLE HEAR AND UNDERSTAND God's grace in all its truth, it totally transforms their lives. We see an example of the transformative power of grace in the lives of people in Colossians 1:3-6. In these verses, we see that grace transforms people's lives by producing faith, hope, love, fruit, and growth. Aren't each of these what a person suffering from addiction needs?

You Need Faith, Hope, and Love
Those suffering from addiction need faith, which is something to believe in. They need hope, which is something to live for and look forward to. They need love, God's love, which is something rely on.

Faith, hope, and love begin healing the hearts of those hurting from addiction, resulting in fruit being produced in their lives. This production of fruit causes spiritual, emotional, relational, and mental growth, totally changing their lives forever.

In the verses at the beginning of the chapter, look closely at what starts this amazing life-change. Colossians 1:6 says this amazing life-change started "*the day you heard it and understood God's grace in all its truth.*" Look closely at how quickly understanding the truth of God's grace began changing people's lives: *the very day they heard and understood God's grace*.

God Wants You To Hear About And Understand Grace

God's heart is for you to hear about and truly understand his grace because he wants you to experience a transformed life. He loves you so much that he does not want you to suffer another day from your addiction. He doesn't want you to suffer another day from guilt, shame, condemnation, self-hatred, depression, and hopelessness. God longs for you to experience freedom by understanding the truth of his grace, which will transform your life.

Since grace is God's power that transforms the lives of people the day they hear and understand it in all its truth, then what is grace? Grace is everything God has freely, fully, and forever done through Jesus to bring you into a love relationship with him, leaving you nothing to do but to accept by faith what Jesus has done.

In the following chapters, we will take a closer look at the transforming truth of grace that God wants you to hear about and understand.

6

God Is Not Counting Your Sins Against You

Blessed are those whose transgressions are forgiven,
whose sins are covered. Blessed is the one
whose sin the Lord will never count against them.
Romans 4:7-8

AS WE EXAMINED IN CHAPTER TWO, God created us to be in a love relationship with himself. However, we chose to walk away from him. Consequently, sin entered the human heart, separating us from God. This separation brought death. God, then, brought grace to the human race through Jesus to reconcile us to himself in a love relationship and restore life to us.

Insight Into Grace
Romans 5:12-21 gives us insight into the unfolding of God's grace to us in Jesus.

> *Therefore, just as sin entered the world through one man, and death through sin, and in this way death came to all people, because all sinned...But the gift is not like the trespass. For if the many died by the trespass of the one man, how much more did God's grace and the gift that came by the grace of the one man, Jesus Christ, overflow to the many! Nor can the gift of God be compared with the result of one man's sin: The judgment followed one sin and brought condemnation, but the gift followed many trespasses and brought justification. For if, by the trespass of the one man, death reigned through that one man, how much more will those who receive God's abundant provision of grace and of the gift of righteousness reign in life through the one man, Jesus Christ! Consequently, just as one trespass resulted in condemnation for all people, so also one righteous act*

resulted in justification and life for all people. For just as through the disobedience of the one man the many were made sinners, so also through the obedience of the one man the many will be made righteous. The law was brought in so that the trespass might increase. But where sin increased, grace increased all the more, so that, just as sin reigned in death, so also grace might reign through righteousness to bring eternal life through Jesus Christ our Lord.

From these verses, we learn the sin of Adam spread to all people, bringing judgment, condemnation, and death. Yet God, in his great love for each of us, brought grace to us through Jesus. Through Jesus, grace overflowed to the entire human race, bringing righteousness and eternal life!

God Demonstrates His Love For Us Through Jesus Dying For Us

The ultimate demonstration of God's love for us was in Jesus dying for our sins. Romans 5:8 says, *"But God demonstrates his own love for us in this: While we were still sinners, Christ died for us."*

In the Garden of Eden, God told Adam that if he ate of the tree, he would die. Yet God, in his loving act of grace through Jesus, paid Adam's and the entire world's death penalty. Rather than each of us paying our own death penalty for our sins and being separated from God, Jesus paid our death penalty so we could have eternal life with God.

God Is Not Counting Your Sins Against You

When Jesus paid our sin penalty through his death, he died for all people and for all sin.

Hebrews 2:9 says:

...by the grace of God he [Jesus] *might taste death for everyone.*

Hebrews 7:27 says:

He sacrificed for their sins once for all when he offered himself.

2 Corinthians 2:14 says:

For Christ's love compels us, because we are convinced that one died for all...

So we see in these verses not only did Jesus, through his love and grace, die for all people, but he also died for all sins.

Through this one act of love and grace, the sins of all people for all time were counted against Jesus, leaving no sins to be counted against any of us.

2 Corinthians 5:19 says: "...*God was reconciling the world to himself in Christ, not counting people's sins against them.*" The question is, "Why is God not counting our sins against us?" The answer is, "Because all of our sins were counted against Jesus. And if all our sins were counted against Jesus, there are none left to be counted against us."

God Has Reconciled You To Himself In A Love Relationship

God's purpose in having all our sins counted against Jesus and no longer counted against us was to remove the barrier of sin preventing him from being in a love relationship with us. By removing the sin barrier, he reconciled us to himself.

> *All this is from God, who reconciled us to himself through Christ and gave us the ministry of reconciliation: that God was reconciling the world to himself in Christ, not counting people's sins against them. And he has committed to us the message of reconciliation. (2 Corinthians 5:18)*

The heart of God is to be in a love relationship with each of us.

But sin separated us from God, keeping us out of a love relationship with him. Yet God, through Jesus, removed the barrier of sin, making it possible for us to be in a love relationship with him.

However, God does not force us into this relationship. Instead, he gives us the freedom to return to this love relationship that mankind walked away from in the Garden of Eden.

> *We are therefore Christ's ambassadors, as though God were making his appeal through us. We implore you on Christ's behalf: Be reconciled to God.* (2 Corinthians 5:20)

We Have A Choice To Make
We have a choice to make. We can choose to accept through faith in Jesus all God has done for us, or we can choose to remain separated from him by rejecting what he has done for us.

It is important to understand that sin is not what separates a person from God. Sin can no longer separate us from God since all our sins were counted against Jesus and God is no longer counting our sins against us. What separates a person from God is the refusal to accept his grace, which he freely offers to us in Jesus. Once someone accepts the grace God has freely offered, he enters into an eternal love relationship with God.

7

All Your Sins Are Forgiven

...God made you alive with Christ. He forgave us all our sins.
Colossians 2:13-14

AS WE CONTINUE TO TAKE A CLOSER LOOK at the transforming truth of grace, it is important to understand God has eternally forgiven all your sins. Colossians 2:13-14 says, "*...God made you alive with Christ. He forgave us all our sins.*"

These two verses clearly teach God has forgiven all our sins. This makes perfect sense. Since Jesus died for all our sins, it only stands to reason he would forgive all our sins.

Forgiven And Alive

Notice the connection between being made alive with Jesus and having all your sins forgiven. Remember, the penalty for sin is death. God told Adam if he ate from the tree he would die. Adam ate of the tree and death spread to all people. So God's goal of grace, in having Jesus die for all your sins, was so you could be made alive again...eternally!

Think about it. If all our sins are not forgiven, then each time we sin we would die spiritually. This means we would become separated relationally from him, with no hope of ever being reconciled to him again. This is why Jesus had to die for all sins, for all people, and for all time. Through his death, the penalty for sin was eternally paid and removed, resulting in eternal forgiveness of our sins and enabling us to be made alive with Jesus. If all our sins are not forgiven, it would be impossible for us to be made alive with Jesus because any unforgiven sin would cause death.

Ephesians 2:1-9 says we were dead in our sins. But through faith in Jesus, God made us alive with him and seated us with him in heaven. This was all done by grace!

If all our sins are not forgiven, then we could not be made alive with Jesus or seated with him in heaven. If there is even one sin that has not been forgiven, then we would become spiritually dead and kicked out of heaven. This is why all our sins have been eternally forgiven!

Your Sins Have Been Eternally Forgiven

The eternal forgiveness of our sins is spoken of in Hebrews 9:12, which says,

> *...by his own blood, thus obtaining eternal redemption.*

Eternal redemption is when Jesus, through his own blood, paid fully and forever the penalty for our sins, thus securing eternal forgiveness. The word redemption means all our sins have been fully paid for and forgiven. Ephesians 1:6-8 says:

> *In him we have redemption through his blood, the forgiveness of sins, in accordance with the riches of God's grace that he lavished on us.*

From these verses, we see redemption and forgiveness are the same. A person can't be redeemed and not forgiven. Redemption and forgiveness mean we have been forever set free from the penalty of sin because Jesus has eternally paid our sin penalty through his blood shed on the cross. Redemption is God's forgiveness which flows abundantly from the grace he has lavished upon us.

What About 1 John 1:9?

When I teach on the eternal forgiveness of sins, which God so graciously lavished upon us in Jesus, I am typically asked about 1 John 1:9, which says, "*If we confess our sins, he is faithful and just and will forgive us our sins and purify us from all unrighteousness."* People ask me if 1 John 1:9 means we must keep asking God to forgive us of our sins each time we sin. This is a good question.

This verse does not in any way tell believers they need to keep asking God to forgive them each time they sin. Rather, it states if we, as unbelieving members of the human race, confess, meaning if we agree with God we have sinned, then God is faithful to do what he said he would do, and he is just in doing what is right, which is to give us the forgiveness Jesus secured through his blood (1 John 1:7; 2:1-2). His faithfulness and justice is based upon what Jesus did for us on the cross.

The truth is that after the cross of Jesus the Bible never tells us to ask God for forgiveness. It does tell us accept by faith the forgiveness God is asking us to receive (Acts 13:38-39; 26:15-18).

1 John Is Not For Believers But Unbelievers

1 John 1:9 is not intended for believers to seek God's forgiveness, but it is for unbelievers to admit their sins and accept God's forgiveness freely given to them in Jesus.

If 1 John 1:9 was meant for believers to continually ask God for forgiveness, then it would be in direct contrast to all the other verses in the Bible following Jesus' death that clearly teach all our sins have been forgiven and God is no longer counting our sins against us. It would also contrast with 1 John 2:12, where John says he is writing to those whose sins have been forgiven.

> *I am writing to you, dear children, because your sins have been forgiven on account of his name.*

John is writing to a group of believers to assure them their sins are forgiven. John knew if the believers he was writing to remained in doubt about God's forgiveness of their sins, because of the false teachers who had invaded this group of believers, telling them all their sins weren't forgiven, then they could never enjoy their relationship with him. So he writes to encourage them with the truth that their sins have been forgiven on account of the name of Jesus who, through his death, paid the sin penalty for us all. If you would like more information on 1 John 1:9, please visit my website, www.simplygrace.info, and click on *The Meaning of 1 John 1:9* in the menu, or read my book, *Forgiven and Cleansed: Understanding 1 John 1:9 In Context.*

In the same way John wrote to those reading his letter, I write to you. If you are experiencing doubt concerning the forgiveness of your sins, I have good news for you! According to the Bible, God is not counting your sins against you. They were all counted against Jesus. All your sins have been eternally forgiven. If there is even one sin we need to ask for God's forgiveness, then all our sins have not been forgiven and God continues to count our sins against us, thus making the Bible contradict itself.

God Wants Us To Accept His Forgiveness, Not Ask For It
The truth of grace is God is not waiting on us to ask him to forgive us. Rather, he is holding out his forgiveness to us, all of it, proclaiming through his ambassadors of grace that he is no longer counting our sins against us. Through his ambassadors, God is asking people to receive his forgiveness by placing their faith in Jesus.

One of these ambassadors was Paul, who we learned about in chapter four. Paul's message, which came directly from the ascended Jesus (Acts 26:15-18), was not one of telling people they need to ask God to forgive them. His message is that God is asking people to accept his forgiveness through faith in Jesus. Here are Paul's own words proclaiming the forgiveness of sins, just as Jesus instructed him:

> *Therefore, my friends, I want you to know that through Jesus the forgiveness of sins is proclaimed to you.*
> (Acts 13:38)

This is that same message I am proclaiming to you.

Relax In God's Grace And Enjoy Your Relationship With God
God wants you to know all your sins have been forgiven. God wants you to know that he is not counting your sins against you. If you do not know all your sins have been forgiven, and God is no longer counting your sins against you, then you can never relax and enjoy your relationship with God. If you have placed your faith in Jesus, you have accepted his forgiveness...all of it! So relax in God's grace. God is not counting your sins against you. All your sins have been eternally forgiven. Enjoy your relationship with God!

8

You Are Not Guilty

There is no difference between Jew and Gentile, for all have sinned and fall short of the glory of God, and all are justified freely by his grace through the redemption that came by Christ Jesus.
Romans 3:22-24

PEOPLE WITH ADDICTIONS carry around heavy feelings of guilt. This guilt consumes them, keeping them trapped in their addiction. However, when a person places his faith in Jesus, God declares that person "not guilty."

God Says You Are Not Guilty
The biblical word for God's "not guilty" declaration is *justified*. The word justified means God has declared you to be innocent of any charge of sin he could ever make against you. He has cleared your sin record and has made you clean in his sight forever. He has declared you not guilty!

Romans 5:1 says, "*Therefore, since we have been justified through faith...*" Romans 3:24, says we are "*justified freely by his grace through the redemption that came by Christ Jesus.*"

The moment you placed your faith in God's payment for your sins through Jesus', God set you free from any charge of sin that he could make against you, declaring you to be innocent before him forever. How could this be?

The Grace Exchange
Your guilt was charged against Jesus. All of it. Jesus took all your guilt upon himself and gave you all his innocence the day you placed your faith in him. This is the great exchange...or as I like to call it, the grace exchange! It is the day when Jesus exchanged his innocence for your guilt by dying for you on the cross, and it is the

day when you exchanged your guilt for his innocence through faith.

Romans 8:31-34 teaches no charge can be made against those whom God has justified.

> *What then shall we say to these things? If God is for us, who can be against us? He who did not spare his own Son but gave him up for us all, how will he not also with him graciously give us all things? Who shall bring any charge against God's elect? It is God who justifies. Who is to condemn? Christ Jesus is the one who died—more than that, who was raised—who is at the right hand of God, who indeed is interceding for us.*

In your addiction, you have lived many days overwhelmed with guilt. Your guilt has led you back into addiction time and time again. But today, God is overwhelming you with his grace, leading you to freedom. He says you are not guilty. He calls you innocent. Believe this truth of grace, you are innocent before God of any charge of sin he could make against you because all your sins were charged against Jesus, and you have placed your faith in him.

God Says You Are At Peace With Him
Since you have been justified by faith in Jesus, you are now at peace with God. Peace with God is different from the peace of God. The peace of God is the absence of worry and anxiety within a person's life that comes from trusting in God. Peace with God is the removal of the judgment and condemnation of God upon a person's sin because this person has received God's grace through faith in Jesus. Through faith in Jesus, God has declared this person innocent of any charge of sin that could be made against him, declaring this person to be clean in his sight. This person is now at peace with God because he is standing in the grace of God. Romans 5:1-2 says:

> *Therefore, since we have been justified through faith, we have peace with God through our Lord Jesus Christ, through whom we have gained access by faith into this grace in which we now stand.*

If you have placed your faith in Jesus, you stand before God in grace. This means you stand before God fully and eternally forgiven of all your sins, innocent and clean before him.

You have stood long enough in the guilt, shame, and condemnation caused by your addiction. Today, start standing in the truth of grace. Stand in the truth you are forgiven, innocent, and clean before God through faith in Jesus.

God Says You Are Clean Before Him

Being clean before God comes from the biblical word *righteous*. It is the result of being justified. The word righteous means that God, in this grace exchange, declared you to be clean in his sight the moment you placed your faith in Jesus. In this grace exchange, Jesus took all your unrighteousness upon himself and then clothed you in his perfect righteousness.

2 Corinthians 5:21 says, *"God made him who had no sin to be sin for us, so that in him we might become the righteousness of God."* This righteousness God provides is his very own righteousness given to us as a gift of grace through Jesus.

> *For if, by the trespass of the one man, death reigned through that one man, how much more will those who receive God's abundant provision of grace and of the gift of righteousness reign in life through the one man, Jesus Christ!* (Romans 5:17)

This gift of righteousness, which God has abundantly provided for us in Jesus, is received through faith. Romans 3:22 says, *"This righteousness is given through faith in Jesus Christ to all who believe."*

God's gift of righteousness is available for all people. This includes you! You may be thinking, because of your addiction, you could never be righteous before God...never clean before God. But I have great news for you. By his grace, God has made a way for you to be righteous.

No one could ever be sinful enough that God's righteousness would not be available to him. No one could ever be good enough for God to declare him righteous. Just as no amount of sin disqualifies a person from receiving God's gift of righteousness, no amount of good works will make a person righteous before God. Since we are all sinful and fall short of the perfect righteousness of God, the only way we can become righteous before God is by receiving through faith his gracious gift of righteousness. If you have placed your faith in Jesus, then you stand before him righteous, just as if you had never sinned!

God Calls You Clean

Addictions make people feel dirty. I am sure you have felt dirty day after day after day because of your addiction. You have tried to become clean, but deep inside you still feel dirty. Not only do you feel dirty, but you believe God and others see you as dirty. This feeling inside you, this belief that God and others see you as dirty, keeps you in bondage to your addiction. The truth of grace is that God calls you clean. God sees you as clean. Begin seeing yourself as God sees you...clean before him, righteous in his sight. Others may still see you as dirty, you may even feel dirty, but God sees you as having a cleared record and as a clean person. You are not guilty!

I know you are having trouble believing this because your feelings tell you the opposite. It seems too good to be true. But it is true. It is grace! I read once that if the gospel you are hearing seems too good to be true, then it is probably the gospel. The good news of this chapter isn't "probably the gospel", it is the gospel...the good news of God's grace freely given to you in Jesus.

Are you addicted to grace yet?

9

You Are Not Under Law But Under Grace

...you are not under the law, but under grace.
Romans 6:14

MANY BELIEVERS LIVE under the law, even though the Bible clearly states in Romans 6:14 that we are not under law but under grace.

> *For sin shall no longer be your master, because you are not under the law, but under grace.*

The Law Reveals Our Need For Grace
In the context of Romans, the law refers to the Ten Commandments. The purpose of the law was to show us our need for grace by educating us about sin, exposing the sin in our hearts, and then executing us for our sin (Romans 3-8).

Romans 1 teaches that all Gentiles (non-Jewish people who weren't given the Ten Commandments but had the commandments written on their hearts), have sinned. Romans 2 teaches that all Jews, (those who were given the Ten Commandments), have sinned. Romans 3 teaches that all have sinned and are unrighteous before God.

Our unrighteousness before God is made known to us by the law so that every mouth may be silenced and the whole world held accountable to God (Romans 3:10-20). However, God provided a way for us to become righteous before him that has nothing to do with the law. This righteousness comes by grace through faith in Jesus. Romans 3:21-26 says:

> *But now apart from the law the righteousness of God has been made known, to which the Law and the Prophets*

testify. This righteousness is given through faith in Jesus
Christ to all who believe. There is no difference between
Jew and Gentile, for all have sinned and fall short of the
glory of God, and all are justified freely by his grace
through the redemption that came by Christ Jesus.

We discover in these verses it is by grace through faith in Jesus
that we have been given righteousness. It was the law that made
us aware of our need for grace by showing us our
unrighteousness. Once the law convinces a person of his sin and
need for grace, thus leading him to faith in Jesus, a person is no
longer under law but under grace.

You Relate To God As Your Father
Under Grace, Not As Your Judge Under Law

Those who have placed their faith in Jesus do not relate to God
under law as their judge, fearing his condemnation. Instead, they
relate to God as their Father under grace, assured of his love,
forgiveness, and acceptance.

By relating to God through grace and not law, Romans
6:14 says sin will not be in control of our lives. Reverse this verse.
If we relate to God through law, sin will be in control of our lives.
One of the keys to breaking free from addiction is to begin
relating to God in grace, where you are assured of his love,
forgiveness, and acceptance. Relating to God in grace is being
confident he has declared you to be forgiven, innocent, and clean
before him. Through this confidence, shame, guilt, and
condemnation begin to fade. And since an addiction is fueled by
shame, guilt, and condemnation, the addiction will begin to lose
its power and control over your life. This is why sin will not be
your master when you live under grace.

You Are Under No Condemnation

Romans 8:1 says there is now no condemnation for those who are
in Christ. The context of this verse is found in Romans 7:7-25,

where the law has proved to someone he has sinned by breaking the Ten Commandments and is deserving of death, leaving him in desperate need of God's grace. This person, then, escapes the condemnation, or punishment, of the law, by embracing God's grace freely given to him in Jesus (Romans 8:1). The good news of grace is that Jesus took upon himself the condemnation for our sins, leaving no condemnation for those who have placed their faith in him.

You do not have to live in the condemnation of your addiction any longer. If you have come to faith in Jesus, there is no condemnation for you, since he took all your condemnation.

The Law Is Good
I do not want you to think the law is bad. It is not. The law is good (Romans 7:7-12). The law works like a mirror by showing us the sinfulness of our hearts and our desperate need for God's grace. The law can do nothing to cleanse our sinful hearts, just as a mirror can never wash someone's dirty face. The mirror can reveal a person's face is dirty but is powerless to wash a person's face. But what the mirror is powerless to do, soap is powerful to do. This doesn't mean the mirror is bad. Rather, it means the mirror is good, since it did what it was designed to do. The law, working exactly like a mirror, shows us our hearts are dirty but is powerless to cleanse our hearts. But what the law was powerless to do, God did through Jesus (Romans 8:3).

Jesus Uses The Law As A Mirror
Anger In The Heart Equals Murder
Jesus used the law as a mirror in Matthew 5:21-22 when he said:

> *"You have heard that it was said to the people long ago, 'You shall not murder, and anyone who murders will be subject to judgment.' But I tell you that anyone who is angry with a brother or sister will be subject to judgment."*

Jesus said being angry in our hearts toward someone is the same as murdering that person with our hands. Why is this true? Because sinfulness is not in our hands but in our hearts. Murdering someone with our hands first starts in the heart. Jesus is showing us our hearts need to be cleansed, not our hands.

Lust In The Heart Equals Adultery

Jesus also used the law as a mirror in Matthew 5:27-28 when he said:

> *"You have heard that it was said, 'You shall not commit adultery.' But I tell you that anyone who looks at a woman lustfully has already committed adultery with her in his heart."*

Here, Jesus says committing adultery doesn't first happen with the body but first happens in the heart. It is not our eyes that are sinful but our hearts. Again, he revealed through the law our hearts are dirty not our eyes.

The Problem Is Our Hearts, Not Hands And Eyes

Many people believe if they obey the law by living morally, they will become righteous, or acceptable to God. Jesus responds to this false belief in Matthew 5:29-30 when he says:

> *"And if your right eye causes you to stumble, pluck it out and cast it from you. For it is better for you that one of your members should perish and not that your whole body should be cast into Gehenna. And if your right hand causes you to stumble, cut it off and cast it from you, for it is better for you that one of your members should perish and not that your whole body should depart into Gehenna."* (Berean Literal Bible)

In these verses, Jesus is identifying the false belief of religious people, which is the belief that by obeying the law, they can become righteous enough to gain eternal life in God's kingdom. Jesus, speaking to those with this false belief, is saying that if this is what they truly believe, then gouge out the eye and cut off the hand that is immoral, so the immoral eye or hand will not keep them from gaining eternal life in God's kingdom. With this reply, Jesus is exposing the absurdity of their false belief.

Our Only Hope Is Grace

Our only hope of having the righteousness necessary to live eternally in God's kingdom is by grace through faith in Jesus. God gives us his righteousness as a gift. We receive the gift of righteousness through faith in Jesus. Once we receive his gift of righteousness through faith in Jesus, we have eternal life in God's kingdom.

> *For if, by the trespass of the one man, death reigned through that one man, how much more will those who receive God's abundant provision of the gift of righteousness reign in life through the one man, Jesus Christ!...grace might reign through righteousness to bring eternal life through Jesus Christ our Lord.*
> (Romans 5:17, 21)

Enjoy Living Under God's Grace

God wants you to understand you are not under law but under grace. He wants you to understand that under grace you are forgiven by him, righteous before him, at peace with him, and under no condemnation from him. As a result, you have eternal life in his kingdom.

Enjoy living under God's grace!

10

The New Covenant Of Grace

And he took bread, gave thanks and broke it, and gave it to them, saying, "This is my body given for you; do this in remembrance of me." In the same way, after the supper he took the cup, saying, "This cup is the new covenant in my blood, which is poured out for you."
Luke 22:19-20

UNDERSTANDING THE NEW COVENANT of grace is essential to becoming addicted to grace. In the Bible, the old covenant of law was given by God through Moses to the nation of Israel, and the new covenant of grace was given by God through Jesus for all people.

> *Out of his fullness we have all received grace in place of grace already given. For the law was given through Moses; grace and truth came through Jesus Christ.* (John 1:16-17)

God's Heart Was To Bless The World
Israel Would Shine God's Love And Goodness To The World
In the old covenant of law, it was God's heart of love to bless Israel, to make them the greatest nation on earth. Then, through Israel, the light of God's love and goodness would shine throughout the whole world, declaring to the nations God is loving and good, and he desires to know and bless the people of the world (Isaiah 49:6).

At this time, the people of the world created false gods and images to worship. They did not know the true God of love and grace. So God formed a nation, Israel, through whom he would reveal himself to the world.

God Created A System Of Blessings And Curses

In order to motivate the people of Israel to walk in a love-relationship with him, so they would not follow after the false gods of the other nations but shine the light of his love and goodness to them, God created a system of blessings and curses based upon the Ten Commandments and other commandments. God told the people of Israel that if they obeyed his commandments, he would bless them abundantly. However, if they disobeyed his commandments, he would curse them (Deuteronomy 28-30).

These commandments, along with its blessings and curses, are what is called the old covenant of law. It was an if-then covenant, meaning that if they obeyed God, he would bless them, and if they disobeyed, he would curse them. It was never God's heart to curse them. God's heart was only to bless them abundantly (Jeremiah 3:19).

God Could Not Bless Israel

Even though God's heart was to bless the people of Israel abundantly, he was never able to bless them. This is because the people of Israel never obeyed God. They lived in constant disobedience to him, experiencing his curses.

This broke God's heart because he loved them and the people of the world so much (Jeremiah 31:3). He wanted to bless Israel not curse them. He wanted Israel to shine the light of his love and goodness into the dark and despairing world.

God Tells Of The New Covenant Through Prophets

To encourage the people of Israel to return to him, and warn them if they didn't, God sent many prophets such as Isaiah, Jeremiah, Ezekiel, and Hosea. Yet they never returned to God. Consequently, they lived under the curses of the law.

While the people of Israel were living under the curses of the law, the prophets foretold of a new covenant. It would be a covenant God would make with the nations of Israel and Judah.

The reason the new covenant would be with Israel and Judah was because Israel had become a divided nation at this time, consisting of Judah and Israel. From this new covenant, not only would Israel be blessed, but all the people of the nations would be blessed as well. Jeremiah 31:31-34 describes the new covenant:

> *"The days are coming," declares the LORD, "when I will make a new covenant with the people of Israel and with the people of Judah. It will not be like the covenant I made with their ancestors when I took them by the hand to lead them out of Egypt, because they broke my covenant, though I was a husband to them," declares the LORD. "This is the covenant I will make with the people of Israel after that time," declares the LORD. "I will put my law in their minds and write it on their hearts. I will be their God, and they will be my people. No longer will they teach their neighbor, or say to one another, 'Know the LORD,' because they will all know me, from the least of them to the greatest," declares the LORD. "For I will forgive their wickedness and will remember their sins no more."*

In The New Covenant, God Remembers Our Sins No More

With the establishment of the new covenant, God would forgive the sins of people, remembering them no more. Through this total forgiveness of sins, people would know God relationally. He would write his law on their hearts, which is the law of the new covenant given to us by Jesus – love one another as I have loved you (John 13:34).

In The New Covenant, God Writes Love On Our Hearts

God would write the law of love on the hearts of his people with his Spirit. Through Ezekiel, he told Israel that he would give them a new heart and would put his Spirit in their hearts (Ezekiel 26:26-27). The Bible refers to God giving people a new heart, a heart containing his Spirit and love (Romans 5:5). Paul calls this a circumcision of the heart done by the Spirit (Romans 2:29).

In The New Covenant, God Begins A Love Relationship With Us

In the new covenant, God would know everyone, from the greatest to the least. The new covenant reveals the true heart of God...his desire to be in a love relationship with all people, no matter who they are...from the greatest of all people to the least of all people.

Jesus Spoke Of The New Covenant

Jesus, when he was gathered with his disciples in the upper room, spoke of the new covenant in Matthew 26:26-27.

> *While they were eating, Jesus took bread, and when he had given thanks, he broke it and gave it to his disciples, saying, "Take and eat; this is my body." Then he took a cup, and when he had given thanks, he gave it to them, saying, "Drink from it, all of you. This is my blood of the covenant, which is poured out for many for the forgiveness of sins."*

Luke 22:19-20 also records the words of Jesus in speaking of the new covenant while with his disciples.

> *And he took bread, gave thanks and broke it, and gave it to them, saying, "This is my body given for you; do this in remembrance of me." In the same way, after the supper he took the cup, saying, "This cup is the new covenant in my blood, which is poured out for you."*

In these verses, Jesus reveals to his disciples he is about to usher in the new covenant of grace, which was promised in the old covenant of law. By giving his body and pouring out his blood, he would take the penalty of sin upon himself for all the people of the world, establishing the new covenant of grace.

The New Covenant Replaced The Old Covenant
The letter of Hebrews explains how the new covenant of grace replaced the old covenant of law (8:7, 10:9). It tells us how the new covenant of grace is better than the old covenant of law. It also tells us how we draw near to God (7:18-22) in a transparent relationship because our sins have been completely and eternally forgiven (9:12).

Where Did Jesus Say The New Covenant Begins?
Jesus Says The New Covenant Begins With His Death Not His Birth
        Jesus told his disciples the new covenant started with his body given for them and his blood poured out for them. In Luke 22:20 he said, *"This cup is the new covenant in my blood, which is poured out for you."*
        The new covenant, or New Testament as we commonly refer to it, does not begin with Matthew 1, as we have been taught. Actually, according to the words of Jesus, the New Testament begins in Matthew 27 with his death. Hebrews 9:16-18 confirms the New Testament begins with the death of Jesus.

> In the case of a will [testament or covenant] *it is necessary to prove the death of the one who made it, because a will is in force only when somebody has died; it never takes effect while the one who made it is living. This is why even the first covenant was not put into effect without blood.*

Forgiveness Under The Old Covenant Was Conditional
Why is it important to understand the New Testament does not begin at Matthew 1? It is important to understand this because people will never be able to accurately interpret the Bible without a correct understanding of the old and new covenants.

Consequently, they will never experience the freedom that is theirs in Jesus.

For example, Jesus says in the Lord's Prayer,

> *For if you forgive other people when they sin against you, your heavenly Father will also forgive you. But if you do not forgive others their sins, your Father will not forgive your sins.* (Matthew 6:14-15)

In these verses, according to Jesus, forgiveness is conditional. If you forgive others, God will forgive you and if you do not forgive others, then God will not forgive you. How are we to interpret this considering the other verses that tell us God is not counting our sins against us, he has forgiven all our sins, and he remembers our sins no more?

Forgiveness Under The New Covenant Is Complete
Remember, both Jesus and the letter to the Hebrews say the new covenant (testament) began when Jesus died. Matthew 6:14-15 are the words of Jesus before he died. At this point in time, Jesus was teaching under the old covenant of law, when forgiveness was conditional. However, under the new covenant of grace, forgiveness is complete.

After Jesus died, the Bible teaches all our sins are forgiven, and we are to forgive one another just as God through Jesus forgave us.

> *Be kind and compassionate to one another, forgiving each other, just as in Christ God forgave you.*
> (Ephesians 4:32)

What we discover in Ephesians, which was written after Jesus died on the cross and established the new covenant, is we forgive others, not to be forgiven by God, but because we are forgiven by God. Remember from chapter four, Paul was taught by Jesus about grace after Jesus ascended into heaven. So Ephesians reflects Jesus' teaching on forgiveness after he established the new covenant of grace in his blood, whereas *The Lord's Prayer* reflects Jesus' teaching on forgiveness before the new covenant of grace was established.

This is so important to understand because a Bible teacher or pastor who doesn't know the difference between the old and new covenants will incorrectly teach these verses, thus putting people back under the condemnation of the law.

Some Bible Teachers Keep People In Their Addiction Through Condemnation

We have discovered addictions are fueled by condemnation. Old covenant law-based teaching, rather than new covenant grace-based teaching, will keep people in their addictions because it will keep people living under the condemnation of the law.

One Teacher Taught We Are Under
The Blessings And Curses Of The Law

Before I was fired from the Christian addiction recovery ministry, which I wrote about in chapter four, I taught thoroughly from Galatians on the new covenant of grace. Galatians teaches we are not under the old covenant of law, with its system of blessings and curses, but are under the new covenant of grace, where we have been freely blessed with every spiritual blessing in Jesus.

While I was teaching we are not under the old covenant of law, living in fear of its curses but hoping for its blessings, another teacher was teaching we are under the old covenant of law along with its blessings and curses. This teacher taught heavily from Deuteronomy 28-29. In my class on Galatians, people were being set free from the law of condemnation, while in his class, they were being placed back under the law, fearing God's curses, but hoping, if they could be religious and moral enough, they would gain his blessings. This is an example of how some Bible teachers and pastors keep people under condemnation and in bondage to their addiction. They teach people to live under the law, rather than setting them free with grace.

A Closer Look At Galatians

Since we were just learning about Galatians, let's take a closer look at Galatians.

Paul wrote Galatians to convince the recipients of his letter they were no longer under the blessings and curses of the law but were free, because of grace, from having to obey the law to become righteous and gain God's acceptance. He wrote this letter because old covenant, law-based teachers infiltrated their churches, convincing them to abandon the new covenant of grace and return to the old-covenant of law. As a result, the Galatian people deserted grace (Galatians 1:6) and were now depending upon the law to make themselves righteous. Paul referred to abandoning grace and returning to the law as "fallen from grace" (Galatians 5:4).

What Does It Mean To Fall From Grace?

Many Bible teachers and preachers teach that to fall from grace means a person has sinned so greatly that they have "backslidden," or moved away from God's favor and back into their old lifestyle of sin. This is possibly what you were taught and have believed.

You believe you have fallen away from God's grace because of your addiction. In reality, you have fallen into grace. Romans 5:20 says that where sin increased, grace increased even more. So according to the Bible, it is impossible to sin so much that a person has out-sinned grace or fallen from grace.

Depending On One's Religious
Activity And Morality To Be Righteous

To fall from grace does not mean a believer has sinned so much that he has backslidden from God and lost his salvation. That is not what the Bible teaches at all. To fall from grace means a person has deserted grace as the means for righteousness and is now depending upon his efforts to obey the law, or his religious and moral behavior, for righteousness. Galatians 5:4 makes this very clear.

> *You who are trying to be justified by the law have been alienated from Christ; you have fallen away from grace.*

Those in this verse had fallen from grace by trying to justify themselves, or make themselves righteous, through their obedience to the Law of Moses. They had not, in any way, backslidden into a life of immorality. It was just the opposite. They were trying to live a life of morality, combined with large amounts of religious activity, thinking their morality and religious activity would earn for them righteousness. In pursuing righteousness through their own moral and religious efforts, rather receiving the gift of righteousness, they were no longer depending upon Jesus and the grace he freely offered. Therefore, they had fallen away from grace.

This doesn't mean they lost their salvation. It simply means they were depending upon themselves for righteousness and not Jesus. They still had faith in Jesus. They still believed in his life, death, burial, and resurrection, but they had been convinced by their religious leaders to return to the law for righteousness. They were still saved, but they set aside grace as the way to relate to God.

If We Can Become Righteous Through The Law, Then Jesus Died For Nothing!

Galatians 2:21 teaches that if a person could gain righteousness by obedience to the law, then Jesus' death was for nothing. That makes perfect sense. Think about it. If morality or religious and church activity make us righteous, then Jesus' death was unnecessary. But the fact is, apart from Jesus, we are all guilty before God and no amount of morality or religious and church activity can make us righteous. Therefore, we need grace.

That is the point Paul makes in Galatians 2:21 when he wrote, "*I do not set aside the grace of God, for if righteousness could be gained through the law, Christ died for nothing!*"

Setting aside grace was exactly what the people of Galatia were doing. They were setting aside grace as the way to become righteous, or accepted by God, and were seeking to gain righteousness through the law. So rather than receiving by faith God's grace and his gift of righteousness, they were seeking to achieve righteousness through the law.

Redeemed From The Law

By returning to the law to earn righteousness, they were obligating themselves to obey the entire law, which no one could ever do, and were placing themselves back under the curses of the law. They were totally ignoring that Jesus, by taking the curse of the law upon himself through his crucifixion, redeemed them from the law and its curses

Galatians 3:10-14 reveals how they had fallen from grace by returning to the works of the law to earn acceptance with God.

> For all who rely on the works of the law are under a curse, as it is written: "Cursed is everyone who does not continue to do everything written in the Book of the Law." Clearly no one who relies on the law is justified before God, because "the righteous will live by faith." The law is not based on faith; on the contrary, it says, "The person who does these things will live by them." Christ redeemed us from the curse of the law by becoming a curse for us, for it is written: "Cursed is everyone who is hung on a pole [tree]." He redeemed us in order that the blessing given

*to Abraham might come to the Gentiles through Christ
Jesus, so that by faith we might receive the promise of the
Spirit.*

Notice what the last verse says, *"He redeemed us in order that the
blessing given to Abraham might come to the Gentiles through
Christ Jesus, so that by faith we might receive the promise of the
Spirit."*

The reason God redeemed us, or set us free from the law,
was so that we could receive the promised Spirit. This is the same
Spirit God promised would come to circumcise our hearts so we
could love and live. The Spirit who comes to live in our hearts is
the Spirit of Jesus. Galatians 4:4-6 says,

*But when the set time had fully come, God sent his Son,
born of a woman, born under the law, to redeem those
under the law, that we might receive adoption to sonship.
Because you are his sons, God sent the Spirit of his Son
into our hearts, the Spirit who calls out, "Abba, Father."*

The Spirit of Jesus Comes To Live In Us

These verses teach us Jesus was born under the law to
redeem people from the law so his Spirit could live in them as
God's sons and daughters, enabling them to call him *"Abba,
Father."* We will look at this verse more closely, as well as the
Spirit-filled life, in chapter eleven.

For now, it is important for us to understand we do not
gain righteousness through the law (moral behavior), or any
religious, spiritual, or church activity, but we are freely given
righteousness as a gift of God's grace, which we receive by faith
in Jesus. It is also important for us to understand that to try to
gain righteousness through morality or religious and church
activity is what it means to fall from grace.

If you have been taught your addiction has caused you to
fall from grace, you have been taught wrong. That is not what the

Bible teaches. The Bible teaches you have fallen into grace. Hold your head up, hold your hand out, receive God's grace. You have not fallen from grace because of your addiction. You have fallen into grace. You have fallen into God's unconditional love, unmerited kindness, unearned blessings, and unlimited forgiveness freely given to you in Jesus.

Live Under Grace

Galatian 5:1 says you were called to be free from the law and to let no one put you under it. Today, start living under grace. Enjoy the freedom of knowing you are loved unconditionally by God and are completely forgiven and accepted by him, and righteous before him by grace through faith in Jesus. Don't let anyone put you under the law or any type of activity, where you must gain God's acceptance (Galatians 5:1).

Eat Of The New Covenant Of Grace

Jesus said for us to eat and drink of the new covenant of grace. As you eat from the new covenant of grace, as you eat of God's forgiveness and righteousness freely given to you in Jesus, as you eat of God's unconditional love, unmerited kindness, unearned blessings, and unlimited forgiveness, you will fill the spiritual hunger inside of you that starves for God's love, forgiveness, and acceptance.

If you would like to read more on the new covenant of grace, I highly recommend Bob George's book, *Jesus Changes Everything*, as well as my own book, *The Story of Grace*.

11

The Spirit-Filled Life

But if you are led by the Spirit, you are not under the law.
Galatians 5:18

IN THE PREVIOUS CHAPTERS, we learned we are not under law but under grace, and the new covenant of grace replaced the old covenant of law. God's ultimate purpose in removing the law and replacing it with grace was so we could know him as our loving Father. Knowing God as our Father was made possible because God sent the Spirit of Jesus to live in us by removing the law. Galatians 4:4-6 says:

> *But when the set time had fully come, God sent his Son, born of a woman, born under the law, to redeem those under the law, that we might receive adoption to sonship. Because you are his sons, God sent the Spirit of his Son into our hearts, the Spirit who calls out, "Abba, Father."*

God Sends The Spirit of Jesus To Live In Our Hearts

These verses teach that the reason God redeemed people from the law was so they could become his loved sons and daughters and so his Spirit could live inside their hearts, enabling them to call God *"Abba, Father."*

In chapter two, we learned from Genesis 3:15 that God's plan was for a male child to be born into the world through a woman. We know this male child was Jesus. Galatians 4:4 tells us Jesus was born of a woman, born under law, to set people free from the law (redeem). He redeemed people from the law so they could be God's sons and daughters, and so he could be their Father. Upon becoming God's sons and daughters, he sent the Spirit of his Son, Jesus, to live in their hearts.

God Cleansed Us From All Sin So Jesus Could Live In Our Hearts

For God to send the Spirit of Jesus to live in us, he had to totally cleanse us. This is because the Spirit of Jesus cannot live in an unclean heart. He totally cleansed us through the cross by his blood. 1 John 1:7 says, *"But if we walk in the light, as he is in the light, we have fellowship with one another, and the blood of Jesus, his Son, purifies us from all sin."*

To walk in the light means we have come into a relationship with God by acknowledging our sin and accepting God's grace by placing our faith in Jesus. The moment we accept God's abundant provision of grace, through trusting in Jesus, our sins are cleansed forever.

Cleansing us from all sins for all time is part of what the new covenant of grace is all about. Hebrews 1:3 says, *"After he had provided purification for sins, he sat down at the right hand of the Majesty in heaven."* When Jesus shed his blood for everyone, he provided purification for all sins, for all people, for all time. It is by faith we receive this purification.

Purification is the act of God where he forgives us of all past, present, and future sins, and declares us to be holy in his sight through the blood of Jesus (Hebrews 10:10, 17-18). The purpose of God in purifying us from all sins is so was he could make our hearts his eternal home. The law showed us our hearts were sinful. God, through the blood of Jesus, cleansed our sinful hearts, and sent the Spirit of Jesus to live in our hearts forever.

I Cleaned My Car So Becky Could Get In It

For God to live in our hearts through the Spirit of Jesus, our hearts had to be completely cleansed. This is because God cannot live in an unclean heart. I remember when Becky, my wife, and I went on our first date. I did what most guys do, I totally cleaned my car. I washed it on the outside and completely cleaned it on the inside. This was because someone special was going to get inside the car, Becky!

Someone special wanted to live inside our hearts, God. But, before he could make our hearts his home, he had to cleanse our hearts. He did this through the blood of Jesus.

A Mother Sterilizes Her Baby's Bottles

Another illustration I like to use when teaching on God cleansing our hearts is a mother sterilizing her baby's bottle. The purpose of a mother sterilizing the bottle is because she is going to put milk or juice in it. In the same way, the purpose of God sterilizing our hearts through the blood of Jesus is so he can live in us through the Spirit of Jesus.

God Cleanses Our Hearts So He Can Live In Our Hearts Forever

The reason God completely forgave all of our sins and cleansed us from all sins was so the Spirit of Jesus could live in our hearts. Think about it. If all our sins are not fully forgiven and our hearts are not completely cleansed, then, the moment we sin our hearts become dirty, forcing God to leave our hearts. Once leaving our hearts, we would die spiritually again, just like Adam and Eve died spiritually in the Garden of Eden. This is why God eternally forgave all our sins and cleansed us from all sins, so Jesus could live in our hearts forever.

If I Have Unconfessed Sin In My Life, Will I Go To Hell?

Tony walked into my office terrorized by fear. He just completed a class at the Christian recovery center where I worked. In this class, he was taught that if he died with any unconfessed sins in his life, he would go to hell. Tony and I talked for a while about how the blood of Jesus purified him from all sin. We looked at verse after verse on the finished, full, and forever work of Jesus on the cross, cleansing him forever from all sin. I explained to him that confession of sin to God was not for the purpose of asking God for forgiveness but was for the purpose of being open and honest with God about everything in his life because of God's love for him.

After talking for a while and studying God's word together, Tony walked out of my office a free man, no longer terrorized by the fear of going to hell if he died with unconfessed sin in his life, but energized by grace, knowing all of his sins were eternally forgiven by God, his heart had been eternally cleansed, and the Spirit of Jesus would never leave him.

God's Plan Was To Make Our Hearts His Home

It has always been God's plan to make our hearts his home by living in us through the Spirit of Jesus. This is why he gives us a new heart. This is the circumcision of the heart by the Spirit spoken of in Deuteronomy 30:6, Ezekiel 36:26, and Romans 2:29.

The Spirit of Jesus in us, as we learned earlier in this chapter, enables us to call God "*Abba, Father.*" Abba is the word Jewish children call their Father. In the United States, we call our father "Dad." In Italy, they call their father "Papa." All of these words reveal a very close, intimate, loving relationship between a Father and his child.

God Wants A Close, Intimate Loving Relationship

A close, intimate, loving relationship is what God desires with each of us. Many verses in the Bible speak of this relationship. 1 John 3:1 says:

> *See what great love the Father has lavished on us, that we should be called children of God! And that is what we are!*

Ephesians 5:1 says, "*Therefore be imitators of God, as beloved children*" (ESV). God's beloved children means we are his dearly loved children for whom he has great affection. Colossians 3:12 says, "*Therefore, as God's chosen people, holy and dearly loved...*"

God is a Father...a Dad...a Papa...who loves you! 1 Corinthians 13:4-8 describes love...God's love for you.

Love is patient, love is kind. It does not envy, it does not boast, it is not proud. It does not dishonor others, it is not self-seeking, it is not easily angered, it keeps no record of wrongs. Love does not delight in evil but rejoices with the truth. It always protects, always trusts, always hopes, always perseveres. Love never fails.

God Is A Loving Father

1 John 4:16 says, *"God is love."* This means God is a Father who is patient and kind, desiring the very best for you. He is a Father who is not angry with you, since all of his wrath toward sin was poured upon Jesus (1 John 2:2). He keeps no records of your wrongs. He does not delight if something bad happens to you. He is not the cause of anything evil or destructive that comes into your life. In his love for you, he wants to protect you, he believes the best for you, and will stay with you through everything you go through. He will never fail to love you and his love will never fail you. He is your loving Dad. He is your loving Papa.

Satan May Have Convinced You
God Doesn't Love You And He Isn't Good

You may have gone through some difficult times in your life, causing you to doubt God's love and goodness. Satan may have convinced you, as he did Eve, that God isn't loving and good. I understand your pain and hurt, many people do.

We live in an evil world. A world that walked away from God's love. Consequently, many people do unloving things that deeply hurt others. You may have been the object of such unloving acts by unloving people.

It is in these hurtful times that Satan seeks to convince you, through his lies, that God is not loving or good. However, the Spirit of Jesus in you wants to lead you into all truth (John 16:13). He wants to set you free with truth. Once you know the truth about God, then the truth will set you free (John 8:32).

The Spirit Wants To Convince You
God Loves You And He Is Good
The Spirit of Jesus in you, the Holy Spirit, wants to make you aware of how much God loves you. Romans 5:5 says, "*...God's love has been poured out into our hearts through the Holy Spirit, who has been given to us.*" Ephesians 3:16-19 says:

> *I pray that out of his glorious riches he may strengthen you with power through his Spirit in your inner being, so that Christ may dwell in your hearts through faith. And I pray that you, being rooted and established in love, may have power, together with all the Lord's holy people, to grasp how wide and long and high and deep is the love of Christ, and to know this love that surpasses knowledge— that you may be filled to the measure of all the fullness of God.*

Through these verses, Paul prays the Spirit, deep inside people's hearts, would strengthen them in their faith to know how much they are loved by Jesus. And, in knowing this love, a love that goes beyond human intellect and directly into the hearts of people, they would be filled with the measure of the fullness of God. This is what it means to be filled with the Spirit (Ephesians 5:18).

The Spirit-Filled Life
The Spirit-filled life is when our faith is strengthened by the Spirit to know deeply in our hearts how much we are loved by Jesus. By knowing how much we are loved by Jesus, we will be filled with the fullness of God's love.

Intoxicated With God's Love
In Ephesians 5:18, Paul compares being filled with the Spirit with the Spirit to being drunk on wine. When people are intoxicated with wine, or any other outside source, they become controlled by whatever intoxicating source is within them. In this

verse, Paul says that instead of being intoxicated with wine, be filled with the Spirit by being intoxicated with God's love.

Whatever we are filled with controls us. If we are filled with anger, anger controls us. If we are filled with bitterness, bitterness controls us. If we are filled with hate, hate controls us. If we are filled with jealousy, jealousy controls us. If we are filled with an intoxicating drug or drink, the drug or drink will control us. If we are filled with the fullness of God's love deep in our inner being, we will be controlled by God's love.

Our hearts being controlled by God's love is how we were created to live. Our hearts were not created to be filled with sin and fear. which is what happened when Adam walked away from God. Instead, it has always been God's plan for our hearts to be filled with his love.

Through the blood of Jesus, God cleansed our hearts. Through the Spirit of Jesus, he brings his love to live in our hearts. The Spirit then guides us into the truth that God is our Father and we are his dearly loved children.

We No Longer Live In Fear But Peace

Because we are loved by God as our Father, we no longer live in fear of his judgment and condemnation. The Spirit of Jesus in us frees us from being afraid of God and fills us with the love of God.

> *For all who are led by the Spirit of God are sons of God. For you did not receive a spirit of slavery that returns you to fear, but you received the Spirit of sonship, by whom we cry, "Abba! Father!" The Spirit Himself testifies with our spirit that we are God's children.* (Romans 8:14-16 - BSB)

Once the Spirit convinces us we are loved children of God, our being afraid of God is replaced with peace.

Romans 8:6 says, *"The mind governed by the flesh is death, but the mind governed by the Spirit is life and peace."* The mind governed by the flesh is referring to the person in Romans 7:7-24 whose mind was at one time controlled by fear of God's judgment and condemnation under the law. But now that grace has come, the Spirit has set this person's mind at peace, because there is no condemnation for those who are in Christ (Romans 8:1). This person no longer lives by the law but lives by the Spirit. Living by the Spirit is living in a peaceful relationship with God as our Father under grace, rather than living in fearful judgment of God under law.

What Does It Mean To Walk By Or Live By The Spirit?
We Call God Our Loving Father

Living in a love relationship with God as our Father is what it means to walk by or to live by the Spirit. Galatians 5:16 says to walk by the Spirit. Galatians 5:25 says to live by the Spirit. Galatians 4:6 says God sent the Spirit of Jesus into our hearts so we can call God our *"Abba, Father,"* *"Daddy, Father,"* our *"Papa, Father."* So to walk by the Spirit or to live by the Spirit is to live every day walking confidently and peacefully in a love relationship with God as our Father.

God Is A Father Who Is Full Of Love For You

What does this love relationship with God as your Father look like? What kind of Father is God? He is full of love for you. He takes joy in you being his child. He brings peace to your heart through his love and grace. He is patient with you. He is kind to you. He is good to you. He is gentle with you. He is faithful to you. This is how he conducts himself toward you every day. This is the very character of God your Father.

The Fruit of The Spirit

The Spirit of Jesus wants to produce the fruit of God's loving nature in your heart so you reflect his love. Galatians 5:22-24 says, *"But the fruit of the Spirit is love, joy, peace, patience, kindness, goodness, faithfulness, gentleness and self-control. Against such things there is no law* (ESV)."

The role of the Spirit is to give revelation of the Father's love to you and produce within you his character. He does this by making you aware of how much you are loved by the Father. As you walk in the love of the Father, the Spirit will begin producing in you the nature of the Father. By experiencing his love for you, his love will flow from within you to others. Your life will be under the control of, or intoxicated with, the Father's love!

Love Doesn't Need A Law

The list of the fruit of the Spirit concludes with, "*Against such things there is no law.*" What does this mean? This means a person whose life is under the influence of God's love, whose life is addicted to grace, does not need the Ten Commandments telling him what to do and what not to do.

Love doesn't need a law. Why not? The reason love doesn't need a law is because love doesn't steal, kill, commit adultery, etc... Love always seeks what is highest and best for the other person. Love is peaceful with people, patient with people, kind to people, forgiving of people, good to people, gentle with people, and faithful to people. Love does not need to be regulated with law nor can it be legislated by law (Romans 13:8-10).

The law is not for those who are walking in the love of the Father under grace, but the law is for those who have never come to faith in Jesus (1 Timothy 1:9). That is why we do not relate to God by the written code of the law, but we live in a love relationship with God through the Spirit.

Romans 7:4-6 says,

> *Likewise, my brothers, you also have died to the law through the body of Christ, so that you may belong to another, to him who has been raised from the dead, in order that we may bear fruit for God. For while we were*

> *living in the flesh, our sinful passions, aroused by the law, were at work in our members to bear fruit for death. But now we are released from the law, having died to that which held us captive, so that we serve in the new way of the Spirit and not in the old way of the written code.*

We Relate To God By The Spirit, Not The Law

Because we are under grace, we don't relate to God through the old way of the written code, meaning the old covenant of law that includes the Ten Commandments. Now that grace has come, we relate to God as our Father through the Spirit.

Our Focus Is On Our Loving Father

Galatians 5:16, says, *"So I say, walk by the Spirit, and you will not gratify the desires of the flesh."* As we walk by the Spirit, in a love relationship with God as our Father, we will not gratify the desires of the flesh. This is because our focus will not be on a false god who is angry with us under law and whose condemnation we think we live under. But our focus will be on God, our loving Father, who has forgiven and cleansed us from all sin, for all time, and who lives in us by his Spirit.

Do Not…!

An illustration I like to use to explain the difference in relating to God in fear as our judge under law and relating to God in love as our Father under grace is a sign on a fence that says "Wet Paint, Do Not Touch!", or a sign that says, "Do Not Look Through The Hole." A person could walk by the fence every day and never think about touching it or looking through the hole. But the moment a sign appears on the fence, prohibiting people from touching it or looking through the hole, our flesh wants to touch it or look through the hole. That is the power of the law.

God Doesn't Want Us Living Focused On His Law

God doesn't want us to live focused on the law. God knows the law only increases sin (Romans 5:20, 7:7-24), putting us in bondage to sin (7:5-6). His whole purpose for the law was to convince us we need grace. God has now set us free from the law, and we relate to him by grace as our loving Father.

Will You Teach My Staff About Grace?
Once I was teaching a class on grace at another Christian addiction and recovery ministry. The leader of the ministry angrily met me after class, telling me I could never come back and teach there again because my teaching on grace would lead people back into their addictions.

He, on the other hand, was teaching the men that if they returned to their addiction after leaving the recovery program, they would lose their salvation and go to hell. I was teaching the men from Scripture that all their sins had been forgiven, they were cleansed of all sin for all time, they were not under the law, and they relate to God as their loving Father through the Spirit of Jesus who, by faith, lives in their hearts.

In my response to the man who told me that what I was teaching would lead the men back into their addictions, I told him that actually what I was teaching would lead them out of their addictions, but what he was teaching would lead them back into their addictions. This made him even angrier!

Then something amazing happened. He calmed down from his anger and began listening to me. It was like the Spirit of God calmed his spirit and opened his heart to listen. The Spirit was desiring to lead him into truth.

I began by giving him an illustration about law and grace using a city dog and a country dog, which I first read about in a book called *Classic Christianity*. I asked the man if he had a dog, which he did. I also asked him if there was a fence around his dog, which there wasn't. He told me that every day his dog was on the porch or in the yard. I asked him what his dog did when he walked out the door or came home from work. He told me that when he walked out the door or came home from work, his dog would jump on him in delight, wanting him to pet him or play in the yard with him.

Think about it. There was no fence. His dog was free to go anywhere. But rather than leaving, his dog stayed on the porch or in the yard.

I asked him what would happen if he built a fence around his dog. The man said his dog would try to dig a hole under the fence, or, if the gate was left open, his dog would run out and possibly run away.

I then explained to him that an owner's love for his dog is the difference between what I was teaching and what he was teaching. I explained to him that what I was teaching the men was like the love he had for his dog. His dog was free to go anywhere, since there was no fence. But because he loved his dog so much, his dog stayed on the porch or in the yard. This love he had for his dog produced delight in the dog every time he went out the door or came home from work.

I compared his love for his dog to God's love for us. I shared with him that if his love for his dog was powerful enough to keep his dog safely at home, then God's love, demonstrated in Jesus giving his life for us, was powerful enough to keep these men safe from their addictions.

In Galatians 2:20-21, we see the power of the love and grace of Jesus to change how a person lives. These two verses say, *"This life I live, I live by faith in the Son of God who loved me and gave himself for me. I do not set aside the grace of God..."* A person who has truly seen the grace of God revealed in Jesus, the one who loved him and gave his life for him, will begin living by faith in Jesus.

In the context of these verses, Paul is saying he no longer lived by the law of God. He was crucified with Jesus. He died to the law. He now lived by faith in Jesus who loved him and gave his life for him.

In staying with the dog illustration. Paul is saying he doesn't live anymore by trying to stay within the fence of the law. No, Jesus tore the law-fence down through his death. Paul now lives on the front porch of and in the yard of God's grace, focused on the love of Jesus and free from the law-fences.

I also told the man that trying to keep these men from returning to their addictions by using the law to control and intimidate them would actually cause the men to return to their addictions. However, teaching the men about grace would empower them to break free from their addictions.

Then suddenly he looked up at me said, "You mean to tell me that what I have been teaching these men has been wrong?" I responded, "That's not what I am telling you, that is what the Bible is telling you." He then said, "So what I teach these men will lead them back into addiction and what you teach them will lead them out of addiction." I said, "Yes." He, then, out of frustration with himself, threw his hat on the ground and said, "Would you teach my entire staff about grace?" Of course I said, "Yes!"

Grace Leads People Out Of Sin

The lie of Satan, promoted through some religious leaders of our day who are opposed to grace, is that grace leads people into sin. Yet, the truth is, grace leads people out of sin.

Jesus used grace to lead people out of sin over and over again. The woman at the well was led out of sin by grace (John g4:1-42). The immoral woman was led out of sin by grace (Luke 7:36-50). Zacchaeus was led out of sin by grace (Luke 19:1-10).

Religious People Hated Jesus Because Of Grace

The religious people of Jesus' day, the Pharisees, hated Jesus for the grace he poured upon people who were in bondage to sin.

They opposed Jesus, trying to suppress the grace that freely flowed from him. They accused him of being light on sin. They accused him of giving people a license to sin. They accused him of participating in sin. I am sure they even called his grace "cheap grace" and "greasy grace," which many religious leaders do today!

Jesus' Response To The Religious People

Jesus, in responding to their self-righteous arrogance and slander, said they were of their father the devil (John 8:44). He told them the truth about themselves, that they were whitewashed tombs, clean on the outside but filthy on the inside (Matthew 23:27). No wonder these religious people hated Jesus and his grace so much. They didn't think they needed grace because they were so proud of their "whitewashed" religious activity and their false sense of morality.

Eventually, to stop this flow of grace, they crucified Jesus. Yet what they didn't understand was their malicious act to suppress grace, once and for all, would be the very act of God that he would use to cause grace to overflow to the entire human race (Romans 5:12-21).

God Will Not Allow His Grace To Be Suppressed

Just like the self-righteous people of Jesus' day opposed grace and tried to suppress the teaching of grace, but couldn't, some people of our day try to do the same. but can't. God will not allow his grace to be suppressed by those who deny the power of grace to change the lives of people. He will not allow them to slander his grace, calling it "greasy grace" and "cheap grace."

Today, something amazing is happening around the world. The Spirit of Jesus is giving the revelation of grace to people all over the world. People in South America, Africa, Asia, and every other continent are learning about and understanding God's grace. Their hearts are overflowing with gratitude to God for his grace (2 Corinthians 4:15). This is exactly what Paul prayed for in Ephesians 1:15-19,

> *For this reason, ever since I heard about your faith in the Lord Jesus and your love for all the saints, I have not stopped giving thanks for you, remembering you in my prayers and asking that the God of our Lord Jesus Christ, the glorious Father, may give you a spirit of wisdom and revelation in your knowledge of Him. I ask that the eyes of your heart may be enlightened, so that you may know the hope of His calling, the riches of His glorious inheritance in the saints, and the surpassing greatness of His power to us who believe.*

The Spirit of Jesus is giving people the revelation and understanding of grace. Their eyes are opening to the riches of God's grace freely, fully, and forever given to them in Jesus!

The Spirit Gives The Revelation And Understanding Of Grace
1 Corinthians 2:10-13 says the Spirit of God searches the deep things of God so the Spirit may give revelation and understanding of what God has freely given us. The Spirit of Jesus lives in believers to give revelation and understanding of grace.

The Spirit Is Giving You Revelation And Understanding
        The Spirit of Jesus in you is giving you revelation and understanding of grace. He is teaching you Jesus paid the penalty for all your sins. He is teaching you God has forgiven all your sins and remembers your sins no more. He is teaching you God has declared you innocent and righteous through faith in Jesus. He is teaching you are no longer under law but under grace. The Spirit is teaching you that God is your loving Father, and he takes joy in calling you his loved son or daughter. He is teaching you your father is patient, kind, good, gentle, and faithful. He is teaching you about the Spirit-filled life.

You Do Not Need To Be "Baptized In The Spirit"

There are some preachers within Christianity teaching people they must be "baptized in the Spirit" or "filled with the Holy Ghost" to be Spirit-filled. They teach the "baptism in the Spirit" is evidenced by speaking in tongues. They tell people that unless they speak in tongues, they are not Spirit-filled. They pressure others to speak in tongues. They surround people at church services, attempting to have them "pray in tongues." They coach people on how to speak in tongues. They make people feel inferior because they do not speak in tongues. They appear spiritually superior to others because they speak in tongues and others do not.

People feel guilty for not speaking or praying in tongues. People feel as if they are missing out on God by not speaking in tongues, as if something is lacking in their lives spiritually.

Those pressuring people to be "baptized in the Spirit" by speaking in tongues have no understanding of what it means to speak in tongues. Biblically, to speak in tongues was an ability given by the Spirit to speak in a language one did not know for the purpose of communicating the truth about Jesus to people whose language they didn't speak. The first use of tongues is found in Acts 2:1-36 when the Spirit enabled the disciples to speak in the languages of those who traveled into Jerusalem from foreign nations. They were enabled to tell these travelers about Jesus in their own languages.

Those pressuring people to speak in tongues have hurt and harmed many people with their religious abuse. I became familiar with this religious abuse while I was teaching weekly at another Christian recovery program. During my weekly teachings, I taught verse by verse through Romans. Those in the recovery program had never been taught the book of Romans and its life-changing message of grace. What they were taught was that they needed to be "baptized in the Spirit" or "filled with the Holy

Ghost" if they wanted to experience all God had for them, and if they wanted to be set free from their addiction.

As I taught this group of hurting people about God's grace, I could see on their faces that their hearts were being healed. They would come up to me after class and tell me how grace was giving them hope and changing their lives.

Because of the response to grace by the people in the recovery program, the leaders asked me not to come back. They were afraid those in the recovery program would be led into a life of sin. Sadly, they continued to pressure the residents to speak in tongues, believing that was the experience they needed to break the power of addiction.

There are some well-known grace pastors who teach that all believers are able to speak in tongues, which they refer to as a "beautiful prayer language." However, I believe their understanding of 1 Corinthians chapters 12-14 is flawed and what they teach is harmful. I don't believe 1 Corinthians 12-14 teach that all people in the Corinthian church had the gift of tongues, which is a gift the Spirit gave to enable people to speak in another earthly language to tell others about Jesus. I believe these chapters teach only some had the gift of tongues and tongues was the least of all the gifts.

Please, if you have never experienced speaking in tongues, do not feel you are missing out on or lacking in something in your relationship with God. You are complete in Christ. You have everything you need in Christ. You do not have to have a certain experience to fully enjoy your relationship with God.

The Spirit-Filled Life Has Nothing To Do With Speaking In Tongues

The Spirit-filled life has absolutely nothing to do with speaking in tongues. People can say they speak in tongues, yet miss out completely on the Spirit-filled life. The Spirit-filled life is walking by faith in a peaceful, loving relationship with God as our

Father, fully convinced we are his forgiven and righteous sons and daughters, who are not under law but under grace, and in whom Jesus lives by his Spirit.

Living Confidently As A Loved Child Of The Father

Today is your day to begin walking confidently and peacefully as God's dearly loved, forgiven, and accepted son or daughter. The Spirit is giving you revelation and understanding deep within your heart to know you are a loved child of the Father.

12

The New Has Come!

"Therefore, if anyone is in Christ, he is a new creation. The old has passed away; behold, the new has come!"
2 Corinthians 5:17

ONE OF THE MOST POPULAR VERSES in Christian addiction recovery programs is 2 Corinthians 5:17 which says, *"Therefore, if anyone is in Christ, he is a new creation. The old has passed away; behold, the new has come"* (ESV). In my conversations with people about this verse, whether those in Christian addiction recovery programs or those in churches, I have not found one person who understands the meaning of this verse in context. This is sad because the power of this verse in the life of one struggling with addiction flows from its true meaning, and the true meaning is discovered in its context.

The Context Of 2 Corinthians 5:17
Paul's Competence In Teaching The New Covenant

The context of this verse begins in 2 Corinthians 3:6 when Paul says, *"He* [God] *has made us competent as ministers of a new covenant—not of the letter but of the Spirit; for the letter kills, but the Spirit gives life."* In this verse, Paul states God enabled him, and those he was in ministry with, to teach with competence the new covenant of grace. His competence is not teaching the letter, meaning the old covenant of law, or the Ten Commandments. Paul says his competence is teaching the new covenant of grace, where a person is declared by God to be righteous, and where the Spirit of Jesus comes to live in that person, freeing him from the law and giving him eternal life.

In 2 Corinthians 3:7-11, Paul writes the following:

Now if the ministry that brought death, which was engraved in letters on stone, came with glory, so that the Israelites could not look steadily at the face of Moses because of its glory, transitory though it was, will not the ministry of the Spirit be even more glorious? If the ministry that brought condemnation was glorious, how much more glorious is the ministry that brings righteousness! For what was glorious has no glory now in comparison with the surpassing glory. And if what was transitory came with glory, how much greater is the glory of that which lasts!

The Old Covenant Of Law Compared
To The New Covenant Of Grace

In these verses, as well as verses 3-6, Paul explains the Ten Commandments, the letters engraved on stone that Moses brought down from Mount Sinai, resulted in condemnation and death. However, the ministry of the new covenant brings righteousness and life. Furthermore, Paul states the ministry of the new covenant of grace is more glorious because it surpasses the greatness the Ten Commandments. In these verses, we also learn the ministry of the new covenant is eternal, compared to the temporal ministry of the letters engraved in stone.

In 2 Corinthians 3:12-16, Paul writes:

Therefore, since we have such a hope, we are very bold. We are not like Moses, who would put a veil over his face to prevent the Israelites from seeing the end of what was passing away. But their minds were made dull, for to this day the same veil remains when the old covenant is read. It has not been removed, because only in Christ is it taken away. Even to this day when Moses is read, a veil covers their hearts. But whenever anyone turns to the Lord, the veil is taken away.

Many Can't See The New Covenant Of Grace

In these verses, we discover a veil covers the hearts of many when the old covenant is read. This means that people can't see that the old covenant brings condemnation and death. Rather, they believe we should continue to live according to the Ten Commandments because they believe the commandments bring life. They do not understand the Ten Commandments, the old covenant engraved in letters on stone, actually bring death (Romans 7:7-24). Only those who have turned to the Lord and are "in Christ" are able to see the old covenant of law brings death and the new covenant of grace brings life (2 Corinthians 3:14-16).

You Have To Be Bold To Teach About Grace

Paul had to be very bold (2 Corinthians 3:12) teaching the new covenant because the law-based people slandered him for teaching the new covenant of grace (Romans 3:8).

Today, teachers of grace must also be very bold. Slander continues from law-based believers who view grace as a license to sin and the law as a guide for spiritual growth. I have been slandered for teaching the new covenant of grace. However, it is important teachers of grace continue to be bold, so we can reach more and more people with the good news of God's grace.

However, in our boldness, we must be gentle, carefully and patiently teaching and refusing to argue with others when they disagree with us as we teach the good news of the new covenant. We must pray God enables them to see the greatness of his grace, since Satan has taken their minds captive, preventing them from understanding the new covenant of grace. This is what Paul told Timothy.

> *Don't have anything to do with foolish and stupid arguments, because you know they produce quarrels. And the Lord's servant must not be quarrelsome but must be kind to everyone, able to teach, not resentful. Opponents must be gently instructed, in the hope that*

God will grant them repentance leading them to a knowledge of the truth, and that they will come to their senses and escape from the trap of the devil, who has taken them captive to do his will. (2 Timothy 2:26-29)

We Reflect The Grace Of Jesus

As we seek to understand 2 Corinthians 5:17, let's continue to examine its context. 2 Corinthians 3:17-18 says:

Now the Lord is the Spirit, and where the Spirit of the Lord is, there is freedom. And we all, who with unveiled faces contemplate the Lord's glory, are being transformed into his image with ever-increasing glory, which comes from the Lord, who is the Spirit.

These verses are also quoted quite often, yet very rarely understood in context. What we see in these verses is when someone turns away from the condemnation and death of the old covenant of law and turns to the Lord in faith, having accepted the gift of righteousness given freely by God in his grace, the Spirit of the Lord Jesus comes to live in this person's heart (see Galatians 4:4-6). When the Spirit of the Lord comes to live in this person's heart, he is set free from the condemnation and death of the old covenant of law. He now contemplates, or deeply focuses on, the greatness of Jesus as revealed in the new covenant of grace. As he contemplates on the greatness of Jesus, the Spirit of the Lord begins to transform him from the inside out into the very image of Jesus. He begins to reflect the grace of God seen in the person of Jesus.

The Spirit Writes On Our Hearts

The Ten Commandments never changed the hearts of people. It only brought condemnation and death. But on the hearts of people who turn to the Lord, the Spirit of the Lord writes the truths of the new covenant of grace (2 Corinthians 3:3). The

Spirit writes that all our sins are forgiven by God, that God is not counting our sins against us, and that he remembers our sins no more. The Spirit also writes we are justified by God, righteous before God, under no condemnation from God, at peace with God, dearly loved children of God, saved forever by God, and have eternal life with God. As the Spirit writes these truths upon our hearts, we begin to reflect the very image of Jesus.

By understanding 2 Corinthians 3, we can now understand 2 Corinthians 5:17 and experience the power of the truth contained in this one verse. Again 2 Corinthians 5:17 says, *"Therefore, if anyone is in Christ, he is a new creation. The old has passed away; behold, the new has come"* (ESV).

As we seek to understand this verse, let's ask a few questions:

1. Who are those who are in Christ?
2. What does it mean to be in Christ?
3. What does a new creation mean?
4. What is the old that has passed away?
5. What is the new that has come?

Who Are Those Who Are In Christ?
In context, which begins at 2 Corinthians 3, those who are "in Christ" are those who have turned away from the condemnation and death of the old covenant of law (the Ten Commandments) for justification and have turned to the Lord. They can now see the surpassing glory of the new covenant of grace and are being transformed into the very image of Jesus by the Spirit as they contemplate the greatness of what the Lord has done for them through grace, and as the Spirit writes on their hearts the truths of grace. Their hearts overflow with thanksgiving because of grace (2 Corinthians 4:15).

They are now new creations, meaning they are recipients of all God has freely done for them in the new covenant of grace through Jesus. Since they are now recipients of the new covenant of grace, they now have a new identity. They are no longer identified with the law, by being under condemnation and death, but are now identified with the new covenant of grace by being forgiven, righteous, possessing eternal life, and having the Spirit of the Lord living in their hearts. The old covenant has now passed away, and the new covenant has now come. This means they are now free from living under the condemnation and death of the letters engraved in stone, the Ten Commandments of law, and now live every day in the surpassing glory of the new covenant of grace as forgiven and righteous people.

What Incorrect Teaching About 2 Corinthians 5:17 Leads To
So often, 2 Corinthians 5:17 is taught in the following way:

> If any person is addicted to drugs, alcohol, etc... and comes to faith in Jesus, he is a new creation. He is now a new person. The old addiction has passed away, and the life without the addiction has come. He used to get drunk, but now he doesn't. He used to do drugs, now he doesn't. He used to watch pornography, but now he doesn't. He used to gamble, but now he doesn't.

This interpretation and application of 2 Corinthians 5:17 misses completely the contextual interpretation and application, thus diminishing the power of the verse. It also causes a misunderstanding of this verse, leading many battling addictions right back into their addictions.

Since I Have Sinful Desires, I Must Not Be A New Creation
      For example, if someone is taught that since he has come to faith in Jesus the old life of addiction is gone and the new life without addiction has come, then, when the desires and cravings

for the addiction return, he assumes he must not really have come to faith in Jesus or be a new creation. He concludes if he had come to faith in Jesus and was a new creation, then he would no longer have those desires and cravings. He then begins living under the law of condemnation and death, experiencing guilt and shame, eventually concluding he has not really come to Christ and is not a new creation. He then, operating from a misinterpretation and application of 2 Corinthians 5:17, returns to a life of addiction, eventually giving up completely.

What Correct Teaching Of 2 Corinthians 5:17 Leads To

If he really understood the truth of 2 Corinthians 5:17 in context, as well as other biblical truths we have looked at in this book and other truths we will look in later chapters, he would not beat himself up with guilt, shame, and condemnation, thus fueling the addiction. Rather, he would live in celebration of God's grace, empowering him to live free from the guilt, shame, and condemnation that fuels the addiction.

This is what happened to Marty. Marty had been in and out of Christian addiction and recovery centers for years. They all taught the same misinterpretation of 2 Corinthians 5:17, which was if a person has come to faith in Jesus, making him a new creation, the old life of addiction is gone and the new life without the addiction has come.

Marty couldn't understand why he continued to battle the sinful desires of his addiction, since he was a new creation in Christ. Therefore, he concluded he must not be a new creation, a true believer in Jesus.

This misunderstanding of 2 Corinthians 5:17 loaded Marty down with guilt and shame. His guilt and shame led him back to his addiction, keeping him there for years.

One day a friend brought Marty to see me. You could see the shame and guilt covering Marty. He had no joy and no hope. We began discussing 2 Corinthians 5:17 and his pain associated with that verse. This broke my heart, since the verse is meant to bring hope not hurt. I explained to Marty the context of 2 Corinthians 5:17, starting in 2 Corinthians 3. As the revelation of the context of this verse came to Marty, the guilt and shame he experienced for years, due to a misunderstanding of the verse, was immediately lifted. Hope and joy suddenly filled his heart as the Spirit wrote the truths of the new covenant on his heart.

When I see Marty now, he beams with joy. He always reminds me his joy and freedom began the day he understood 2 Corinthians 5:17 as he and I talked about the context and correct interpretation of this verse. Today, Marty tells many people about the transformation that took place in his heart the moment he understood 2 Corinthians 5:17 in context.

What Does Being A New Creation In Christ Really Mean?

If you have come to faith in Jesus, you are a new creation in Christ. You have a new identity. You are a person who is forgiven and righteous. God is not counting your sins against you. You are reconciled to God. The Spirit of Jesus lives in you. The old covenant of law, bringing condemnation and death, has gone. The new covenant of grace, bringing righteousness, forgiveness, and life has come.

This does not mean you will never desire your addiction again. It simply means you no longer relate to God in the old way, through the guilt and condemnation of the Ten Commandments. You now relate to God in a new way, through the forgiveness and righteousness of the cross, where grace overflows to you.

The Spirit of the resurrected and ascended Jesus now lives in you, bringing you eternal life and replacing the law, which brought death. His Spirit convinces you are forgiven and righteous, a possessor of eternal life. It is this understanding that will help you overcome the addiction when the desires of the addiction surface.

13

You Are Saved

For it is by grace you have been saved, through faith—and this is not from
yourselves, it is the gift of God— not by works,
so that no one can boast.
Ephesians 2:8-9

THERE ARE SOME BIBLE TEACHERS and preachers today who teach that people can lose their salvation. They teach this is out of unbelief, fear, pride, and ignorance. Out of unbelief, because they do not believe the grace and love of God freely given to us in Jesus is powerful enough to change someone's heart and life. Out of fear, because they are afraid people will use grace as a license to sin. Out of pride, because they believe they are more righteous and moral than others and would never use grace as a license to sin like others would. And finally, out of ignorance, because they simply are ignorant of God's word, constantly teaching verses out of context and using these verses to threaten people with the loss of salvation or to make them doubt they were ever saved, should they struggle with sinful desires or cravings brought on by the addiction.

This misuse of God's word by Bible teachers and preachers actually keeps people in bondage to their addictions. Only by understanding they are eternally saved by grace through faith in Jesus can they ever be strengthened internally to break free from their addiction.

Grace Teaches Us To Live Good Lives
Grace Creates An Eagerness Within Us

Understanding that you are saved and what it means to be saved are vital in breaking free from your addiction. The Bible speaks over and over again about how grace motivates us to do good. For example, Paul, in writing to Titus, describes how grace educates us about how to live moral and upright lives, creating an eagerness within us to do good.

> *For the grace of God has appeared that offers salvation to all people. It teaches us to say "No" to ungodliness and worldly passions, and to live self-controlled, upright and godly lives in this present age, while we wait for the blessed hope—the appearing of the glory of our great God and Savior, Jesus Christ, who gave himself for us to redeem us from all wickedness and to purify for himself a people that are his very own, eager to do what is good.* (Titus 2:11-14)

Grace Motivates Us

In Titus 3:3-8, Paul again writes about how grace motivates us to do good.

> *At one time we too were foolish, disobedient, deceived and enslaved by all kinds of passions and pleasures. We lived in malice and envy, being hated and hating one another. But when the kindness and love of God our Savior appeared [grace], he saved us, not because of righteous things we had done, but because of his mercy. He saved us through the washing of rebirth and renewal by the Holy Spirit, whom he poured out on us generously through Jesus Christ our Savior, so that, having been justified by his grace, we might become heirs having the hope of eternal life. This is a trustworthy saying. And I want you to stress these things, so that those who have trusted in God may be careful to devote themselves to doing what is good. These things are excellent and profitable for everyone.*

Grace Moves Us

Paul, in writing to Timothy, says that grace moves us to

live a holy life, meaning a life of moral purity and love.

> *He has saved us and called us to a holy life—not because of anything we have done but because of his own purpose and grace. This grace was given us in Christ Jesus before the beginning of time, but it has now been revealed through the appearing of our Savior, Christ Jesus.* (2 Timothy 1:9-10)

Grace Produces Good Works Within Us

Grace is the power of God that produces good works through us.

> *For by grace you have been saved through faith. And this is not your own doing; it is the gift of God, not a result of works, so that no one may boast. For we are his workmanship, created in Christ Jesus for good works, which God prepared beforehand, that we should walk in them.* (Ephesians 2:8-10)

From these verses in Ephesians, we see grace not only secures our salvation, but also produces good works in us. These good works are the works of grace "*which God prepared beforehand, that we should walk in them.*"

The "we" of the verse "we are his workmanship" are those who have received his grace. By receiving his grace, we become his workmanship in Christ. God begins to work his good work of grace in and through us. These good works of grace were prepared by God before we were ever born. So grace is not only the power securing our salvation, but, as we have learned, grace also produces good works in and through us which God prepared before we were ever born.

Some Bible Teachers See Grace Differently Than God

Unfortunately, some Bible teachers and pastors who believe the teaching of grace leads to immorality and who accuse grace teachers of giving people permission to sin do not see grace the way God sees grace. God sees grace differently. God sees grace as his power that produces his good works in and through people, while they see grace as the power that leads people into sin.

Doesn't The Bible Say Be Holy For I Am Holy?

Often, when I teach on grace, some people, in a prideful, self- righteous manner, ask me: "Doesn't the Bible say we should be holy for God is holy?" I always respond, "Yes, that is what the Bible says." Then I ask, "Do you know where this verse is in the Bible and what the context is?" Not one person asking the question has known the context. They may know where this verse is in the Bible, but they don't know the context. This verse is found in 1 Peter 1:15-16.

> But just as he who called you is holy, so be holy in all you do; for it is written: "Be holy, because I am holy."

The Context Is Grace!

The context of these verses is all about God's grace. 1 Peter 1:10-12 says:

> Concerning this salvation, the prophets, who spoke of the grace that was to come to you, searched intently and with the greatest care, trying to find out the time and circumstances to which the Spirit of Christ in them was pointing when he predicted the sufferings of the Messiah and the glories that would follow. It was revealed to them that they were not serving themselves but you, when they spoke of the things that have now been told you by those who have preached the gospel to you by the Holy Spirit sent from heaven. Even angels long to look into these things. Therefore, with minds that are alert and fully sober, set your hope on the grace to be brought to you when Jesus Christ is revealed at his coming.

The grace Peter refers to in 1 Peter chapter one is about the salvation spoken of by the prophets in the Old Testament when the Spirit of Jesus in them told of his coming into the world as the Messiah, or King, to establish his kingdom of love, joy, peace, healing, and wholeness.

In this kingdom, the world will no longer live in chaos, being hurt by and hurting one another. In this kingdom, there will be no more death, deformity, or disease. There will be no hunger. There will be no more terrorism or wars. In this kingdom, the people of the world will live in love. Peace will flow all over the world. I write about this coming kingdom in my book, **The Story of Grace**.

Peter writes that the prophets spoke of the sufferings of the Messiah, this coming King, before the glories of his kingdom would be realized. The sufferings of the King refer to his death. The prophets searched intently to know more about God's grace to come and when the King would usher in this kingdom of grace.

What we learn from the Old Testament prophets is a Messiah, a King, was coming into the world. He would wear a crown as King, bringing peace all over the world. He would bear a cross as Savior, bringing forgiveness to people all over the world. The prophets, looking ahead to the grace to come, did not understand all that we understand. They knew the Messiah would die, according to Isaiah 53, and rise from the dead, according to Psalm 16:10. But they did not understand, as we do, that his death would come through the cross.

Peter even says the angels long to look into "these things," meaning they long to look into the grace of God coming into the world through the Messiah.

Peter, in 1 Peter 1:3-5, delightfully celebrates this coming kingdom of grace and our eternal enjoyment of it. In 6-9, he speaks of the difficulties we will go through on this earth before Jesus comes as King and establishes his kingdom. Yet, he writes, these difficulties on earth will refine our faith, a faith that is of greater worth than gold. Peter says we are filled with inexpressible and glorious joy as we await by faith for this coming kingdom.

Grace: The Motivation For Living A Holy Life

Peter, in joyful anticipation of this King who is coming to establish his kingdom of grace, writes in verse 13 for us to have sober minds, meaning minds not intoxicated with Satanic and worldly lies about how to live, but minds that think soundly and morally. He writes for believers not to conform to the evil desires of the world, which they had before being told about the King of grace and his coming kingdom of grace, but to live holy lives on earth, meaning lives of moral purity and love, as we await this coming King and kingdom.

So we see in 1 Peter 1:3-16 the motivation for living a holy life comes from the inspiration of grace. Self-righteous legalists, who are so afraid someone might use grace as a license to sin, never bother to teach about God's grace. It never occurs to them grace is the inspiration for living a holy life. Instead, taking verses out context, as exemplified by their constant prideful quotation of the verse "Be holy as I am holy," they seek to intimidate people through fear to live a holy life rather than inspire them by grace.

A Closer Look At Eternal Salvation

One of their intimidation tactics is threatening people with the loss of their salvation. As I wrote earlier in the chapter, this threat actually keeps people in bondage to their addictions, rather than setting them free from their addictions. So let's take a closer look at the eternal security of our salvation.

Salvation Is By Grace Through Faith

Ephesians 2:8-9 says:

*For it is by grace you have been saved, through faith—
and this is not from yourselves, it is the gift of God— not
by works, so that no one can boast.*

These verses make it very clear salvation is not earned through works, meaning religious activity and morality, but is given to us as a gift of God's grace. It is received by faith.

These are verses I became familiar with early in my Christian experience. However, I never knew their context. It never occurred to me to study these verses in context, until I started my grace journey in 1991. After understanding the context, Ephesians 2:8-9 played a significant role in my spiritual growth.

Salvation Is Being Resurrected From The Dead

The immediate context of these verses begins in Ephesians 2:1 by saying, *"As for you, you were dead in your transgressions and sins."* This is what salvation is all about, bringing the dead to life. When Adam ate from the tree, death entered the human race, spreading to all people, for all have sinned (Romans 5:12). So God, in bringing salvation to us, was actually saving us from spiritual death, or separation from him. Salvation is God resurrecting us from the dead. He accomplished this by grace through Jesus.

We have already looked at Genesis 3:15 where God said a male child would come into the world, crushing the head of Satan. We know this male child is Jesus. Jesus brought life into our dead world through grace. Bringing life to the world by giving us grace in Jesus was God's plan before time began (2 Timothy 1:9-10).

God's plan to bring grace to the world unfolded through Abraham and Sarah. Through Abraham and Sarah, the nation of Israel was formed. It was through Israel that Jesus was born, bringing life to the world through grace.

Before Abraham's name was Abraham, it was Abram. Before Sarah's name was Sarah, it was Sarai. God changed

Abram's name to Abraham and Sarai's name to Sarah. Notice in the 5th letter of both their names the letter "h" replaced the letter that was previously there. In Abram's name, the "m" was replaced with "h". In Sarai's name, the "i" was replaced with "h". The letter "h" in the Hebrew language means "divine breath," and the number "5" in the Hebrew language means "grace." By using the letter "h" in the 5th letter of their names, God was revealing to the world he would breathe life back into the human race through grace.

In the beginning, God breathed life into mankind (Genesis 2:7). However, when Adam sinned, the life God breathed into mankind died, leaving mankind in need of the restoration of life. God's plan was to breathe life, eternal life, back into mankind through Jesus by grace.

> *This grace was given us in Christ Jesus before the beginning of time, but it has now been revealed through the appearing of our Savior, Christ Jesus, who has destroyed death and has brought life and immortality to light through the gospel.* (2 Timothy 2:9-10)

> *For if, by the trespass of the one man, death reigned through that one man, how much more will those who receive God's abundant provision of grace and of the gift of righteousness reign in life through the one man, Jesus Christ!* (Romans 5:17)

> *...so that, just as sin reigned in death, so also grace might reign through righteousness to bring eternal life through Jesus Christ our Lord.* (Romans 5:21)

> *For the wages of sin is death, but the gift of God is eternal life in Christ Jesus our Lord.* (Romans 6:23)

As these verses indicate, salvation is the restoration of life by grace through Jesus. We can never truly reign in life, or enjoy life to its fullest, until we receive God's grace. When we receive God's grace, it reigns in us and brings eternal life to us. This removes the fear of losing our salvation and replaces it with the fullness of joy because we know we have eternal life.

Salvation Is Being Seated With Christ

Ephesians 2:1 says we were dead in our transgressions and sins. Ephesians 2:2-3 says we were objects of God's wrath (God's loving judgment when he removes all sin and sinners from the earth) because of our sinful behavior. However, from Ephesians 2:4, we learn about the greatness of God's love for us and the richness of his mercy to us.

> *But because of his great love for us, God, who is rich in mercy...*

In the greatness of his love and the richness of his mercy, God made us alive with Jesus and seated us with him in heaven itself!

> [God] *made us alive with Christ even when we were dead in transgressions—it is by grace you have been saved. And God raised us up with Christ and seated us with him in the heavenly realms in Christ Jesus.*

We see that salvation, in the context of Ephesians chapter two, is when God, because of his great love for us and grace and mercy to us, rescued us from his wrath, resurrected us with Jesus from the dead, and made us residents of heaven itself by seating us with Jesus.

We Can't Bring Ourselves Back To Life

We had nothing to do with this saving grace. God gave us this grace in Jesus before time began, while we were still dead in our sins. That is why Ephesians 2:8-9 says, *"For it is by grace you have been saved, through faith—and this is not from yourselves, it is the gift of God— not by works, so that no one can boast."*

Just as a physically dead person cannot bring himself back to life, neither can a spiritually dead person. Bob George, in his book, *Classic Christianity*, says two things must happen if a dead man is to be brought back to life. First, whatever killed him, let's say a disease, must be cured. Second, life must be breathed back into him. If life is breathed back into him without curing the disease, you have only a living person who will die again. Bob goes on to write in his book that if you cure his disease but do not breathe life back into him, you have a healthy dead man. So to really bring a dead person back to life, the disease must be cured and life must be breathed back into him.

God Brought Us Back To Life

This is what God did for us spiritually. Through grace, he cured our disease of sin by having Jesus die for us. God, then, forgave us all our sins.

> *...to the praise of his glorious grace, which he has freely given us in the One he loves. In him we have redemption through his blood, the forgiveness of sins, in accordance with the riches of God's grace that he lavished on us.* (Ephesians 1:6-8).

Through the resurrection and ascension of Jesus, God breathed life into us by sending the Spirit of Jesus to live in our hearts.

The Resurrection Power Of Grace

Paul prayed the Spirit would give the believers in Ephesus wisdom and revelation so they would know God the Father more deeply and the riches of his grace more fully.

> *I keep asking that the God of our Lord Jesus Christ, the glorious Father, may give you the Spirit of wisdom and revelation, so that you may know him better. I pray that*

the eyes of your heart may be enlightened in order that
you may know the hope to which he has called you, the
riches of his glorious inheritance in his holy people...
(Ephesians 1:17-18)

Paul compared the riches of God's grace to the power of the resurrection and to the ascension of Jesus into heaven, where he was seated at God's right hand. Paul prayed they would know the power of God's grace in their lives.

...and his incomparably great power for us who believe.
That power is the same as the mighty strength he
exerted when he raised Christ from the dead and seated
him at his right hand in the heavenly realms...
(Ephesians 1:19-20)

In these two verses, we see that nothing compares to the power of God's grace, except the mighty strength of God that raised Jesus from the dead and seated him heaven. Paul says the power of God's grace *"is the same as the mighty strength he exerted when he raised Christ from the dead and seated him at his right hand in the heavenly realms."*

He writes in Ephesians 2:7 about *"...the incomparable riches of his grace..."* Nothing, but the resurrection, compares to the power of God's grace!

Paul prayed in Ephesians 1:18 that the eyes of the believers' hearts *"would be enlightened so that you may know what is the hope to which he has called you, what are the riches of his glorious inheritance in the saints."* Paul knew an internal revelation of grace by the Spirit in the hearts of people would powerfully change their lives.

The Hope Of Grace
Experiencing the powerful riches of grace freely given to them in Jesus was the hope to which they were called. Hope in this verse

is not wishful thinking. Rather, it is absolute assurance by God himself that all his grace has been freely and abundantly given to us in Jesus.

My Prayer For You
My prayer for you is the Spirit would open the eyes of your heart to see the riches of God's grace freely and abundantly poured out for you through Jesus for all your sins. I pray you would see with the eyes of your heart the greatness of God's love for you and the richness of his mercy to you so you can know him better. I pray, through the opening of your eyes by the Spirit to God's grace, love, and mercy, that you would experience his life-changing power. I pray grace becomes such a powerful force in your life that the only way you can explain to others the life-changing power of grace is by saying, "I am addicted to grace!"

The Joy Of Grace Will Be With Us For All Eternity
One amazing fact to know about grace is that the joy grace produces in our hearts and minds while on the earth will be with us for all eternity. Ephesians 2:6-9 says:

> *...it is by grace you have been saved...in order that in the coming ages he might show the incomparable riches of his grace, expressed in his kindness to us in Christ Jesus. For it is by grace you have been saved, through faith...it is a gift of God...*

The joy that comes from knowing we are saved eternally will never end. In the coming ages, referring to when Jesus returns as King to establish his eternal kingdom on earth (Ephesians 1:9-10, 21), the gift of God's grace will be on full display for everyone to experience and enjoy! For all eternity, we will experience and enjoy the free gift of salvation given to us through the kindness of God in Jesus. For all eternity, we will be in awe of the grace of God. For all eternity, we will be addicted to grace, experiencing its joy forever!

Boasting In Jesus
In the coming ages, as we live joyfully in the Kingdom of Grace, there will be no boasting, because no one's religious activity or morality qualified them for entrance into his kingdom. Our only boasting will be in Jesus, the King of the kingdom who wears the crown. We will boast in the King who became our Savior by bearing the cross, qualifying us to live as citizens in his Kingdom of Grace! Colossians 1:12-14 says:

> *... giving thanks to the Father, who has qualified you to share in the inheritance of the saints in the light. For he has rescued us from the dominion of darkness and brought us into the kingdom of the Son he loves, in whom we have redemption, the forgiveness of sins.*

God Wants You To Live Eternally In His Kingdom
Living eternally in God's kingdom is what eternal life is all about. Nicodemus, a Pharisee, came to Jesus one night to ask him how one could enter the kingdom of God. Jesus told him he must be born of the Spirit. The way he would be born of the Spirit would be by believing. Jesus told him:

> *For God so loved the world that he gave his one and only Son, that whoever believes in him shall not perish but have eternal life. For God did not send his Son into the world to condemn the world, but to save the world through him.* (John 3:16)

Salvation, eternal life, and living in the Kingdom of God are synonymous terms. God loves everyone in the world with a deep passion. No matter who they are or what they have done, he wants them to live eternally in his kingdom. The only way to enter God's kingdom of grace is by believing in Jesus.

Prostitutes And Tax Collectors

During Jesus' time on earth, the first ones who were entering the kingdom of God were the prostitutes and tax collectors. According to Jesus, they were entering the kingdom ahead of the Pharisees. (Matthew 21:31). This is because the Pharisees thought entering the kingdom came through their religious activity and morality. Yet, in reality, entering God's kingdom came through repentance (Matthew 21:31-32).

Grace Creates Repentance And Produces Life-Change

Typically, repentance is taught as turning from sin and promising God we will try harder not to sin. People are taught they "need to repent of every sin." Their view of God is a god who stands ready to punish them, rather than ready to pour his grace upon them. This understanding of repentance always leaves out the good news of God's grace revealed in his kindness to us in Jesus. This is sad, because it is the grace of God revealed in his kindness to us in Jesus which creates repentance in the heart of a person, producing life-change (Romans 2:4).

God Is Gracious And Compassionate

In the Old Testament, the people of Israel lived in continual rebellion to God. Yet God continually reached out to them with a gracious and compassionate heart, passionately desiring they return to him.

King Hezekiah sent word to the people of Israel, appealing for them to return to God because "*he is gracious and compassionate*" (2 Chronicles 2:9). Nehemiah, in calling for Israel to return to God, speaks of God's gracious and compassionate heart toward rebellious Israel (Nehemiah 9:17, 31). Isaiah speaks of the longing in God's compassionate heart to be gracious to Israel, standing ready to pour out his grace upon them when they cry out for help (Isaiah 30:18-19).

The reason Jonah did not want to go to Nineveh, a ruthless

nation, was because God is a gracious and compassionate God (Jonah 4:2). Jonah, knowing God was gracious and compassionate, ran from God, because he wanted the Ninevites to pay for their sins rather than for God to pour grace upon them in their sins.

So we see, that even in the Old Testament, where God related to Israel through the law, he consistently reached out to them in grace. Yet they refused his grace.

Can't Leave Out Grace And Teach Repentance

Anyone who claims to be teaching biblical repentance but leaves out the gracious compassionate heart of God as the motivation for repentance is not teaching repentance. Again, it is God's gracious and compassionate heart that creates repentance and produces life-change.

During his time on earth, Jesus embodied the gracious and compassionate heart of God toward those in need of repenting, which was everyone.

Repentance is an act of faith in Jesus where a person, in response to the kindness and grace of God flowing through Jesus, admits his sins and accepts, through faith in Jesus, God's grace.

The Pharisees refused to respond to God's grace in repentance because they were so proud of their religious activity and morality (Matthew 21:32, 23:1-36). Rather than responding to his grace in repentance, the Pharisees rejected God's grace by viciously opposing Jesus as he lavished grace upon those who were aware of their sins and were ready to accept his grace.

The people who were responding to God's grace in repentance were the prostitutes and tax collectors. When they responded to God's grace through faith in Jesus, his grace powerfully changed their lives. They became addicted to grace!

Lives Changed By Grace
Matthew And Zacchaeus Received God's Grace

Intoxicated with grace, Matthew left his tax collector's booth and became a disciple of Jesus. Because of Matthew's influence, many other tax collectors left their lives of thievery and deception. Even Zacchaeus, the chief tax collector, was influenced by Matthew and the other tax collectors as he saw empty tax booths, once occupied by tax collectors, now vacated because of grace.

These former tax collectors' addiction to grace so affected Zacchaeus' life that he realized how desperate he was for grace. Living in shame and guilt because of his life, he climbed up a tree just to get a glimpse of the one who was full of grace, Jesus. Jesus, knowing he was in the tree, and knowing his desperate need for grace, walked up to Zacchaeus, and then went to Zacchaeus' home.

I am sure Zacchaeus poured his heart out to Jesus...his pain...his guilt...his shame. I am sure Jesus listened with a heart of grace and lavished grace upon Zacchaeus. This encounter with grace so impacted his life that Zacchaeus became addicted to grace. Under the influence of grace, he went back to all the people he had stolen money from and paid them back double. Zacchaeus had become addicted to grace!

Mary, The Sister Of Martha, Received God's Grace

Another person who responded in repentance to the grace of Jesus was the immoral woman. More than likely she was a prostitute living on the streets of her town and suffering in shame and guilt from her lifestyle. Seeing her need for grace, she approached Jesus while he was having dinner inside the home of a Pharisee. Weeping at the feet of Jesus, she received God's grace that flowed abundantly from the heart of Jesus. His grace forgave her sins and freed her from guilt and shame. His grace empowered her to leave her miserable life of prostitution. She became addicted to grace! (Luke 7:36-50)

In John 11:2, we discover who this woman is, she is Mary,

the sister of Martha. In Luke 10:38-42, we find her sitting at the feet of Jesus, listening to and learning from him. This is the same Mary who at one time wept at the feet of Jesus because of the guilt of her sin but is now sitting at the feet of Jesus because of the grace lavished upon her in her sin.

What Good Thing Must I Do?

Once, a wealthy man came to Jesus and asked him what good thing must he do to inherit eternal life (Matthew 19:16-22). Jesus responded by telling him to obey the commandments if he wanted to enter the kingdom of heaven. The man replied he had obeyed all the commandments since he was a child. Jesus told him to sell everything he had and give to the poor, then he could be saved. With this, the man went away sad.

In this exchange between Jesus and the rich man, we see that eternal life, living in the kingdom of heaven, and being saved are all the same. The man thought entrance into the kingdom was through the good works of the law. Jesus quickly exposed the sin in his heart by holding the law up like a mirror to show the man the sin in his heart. Once the man saw the sin in his heart, he went away sad rather than receiving God's grace.

Jesus' disciples responded by asking Jesus who could be saved, since this man tried sincerely to obey the law from childhood. Jesus replied that what is impossible with man, saving ourselves through good works, is possible with God...with grace. Even though a person could never be good enough to enter God's eternal kingdom, the grace of God enables the "worst" of people to enter his kingdom...such as the tax collectors and prostitutes.

God's Grace Is Powerful

It is God's heart that all be saved and not perish. He patiently waits for people to believe and receive his grace (2 Peter 3:9). When people receive his grace through faith in Jesus, we see the power of his grace to change their lives.

God's Grace Changes How We Live

The life-changing power of grace is seen in Ephesians 2:1-2:

> *"As for you, you were dead in your transgressions and sins, in which you used to live when you followed the ways of this world..."*

In Ephesians 2:10, those who experience the life-changing power of grace will walk, as they grow in grace, in the good works God prepared in advance for them. In Ephesians 3:20-21, we see the power of God's grace doing more in a person's life than he could have ever asked or imagined.

God's Grace Saves Us Forever

God's grace is powerful. It saves us for all eternity. Notice in Ephesians 2:8 where Paul says, *"...you have been saved..."* Salvation is permanent. Salvation is eternal life. If people could lose their salvation, then they would have to be made "unalive" in Jesus, kicked out of heaven, and be "unforgiven" of all their sins. Salvation was never gained through behavior and cannot be lost through behavior. Salvation is given as a gift of God's grace. It is not bestowed upon us by good behavior. It cannot be withdrawn from us through bad behavior. If it could, then it never was a gift, and it was never eternal.

If you have come to faith in Jesus, you are eternally saved. You have been forgiven of all your sins, made alive with Jesus, seated with him in heaven, and are a permanent citizen of his kingdom.

Some Believe God's Grace Isn't Powerful

The teaching that we can never lose our salvation unfortunately scares some Bible teachers and preachers. This is because they believe the gospel, or the good news of God's grace, is not powerful enough to change a person's heart and life. Rather than believing the teaching of God's grace powerfully change people's lives, they are fearful the teaching about grace will give people a license to sin.

They Take Verses Out of Context

Because grace frightens these Bible teachers and preachers, they take many verses out of context in order to terrorize believers with the false teaching they can lose their salvation.

One example of this is found in Hebrews 10:26-27 which reads:

> *"If we deliberately keep on sinning after we have received the knowledge of the truth, no sacrifice for sins is left, but only a fearful expectation of judgment and of raging fire that will consume the enemies of God."*

They use this verse to scare believers with the loss of salvation if they do not behave morally. Immediately, when they see the word "sinning," they automatically view this word as immorality. However, by properly studying the book of Hebrews, we discover that sin, in the book of Hebrews, is a hardened, unbelieving heart that rejects resting in the new covenant of grace, the finished work of Jesus, and instead, continues to seek a right standing with God through the works of the law (Hebrews 3:1-4:11).

They Have a Hardened Heart

This is the same sin many Bible teachers and preachers are committing today. They have sinful, hardened, unbelieving, and disobedient hearts that refuse to rest by faith in the finished work of Jesus. Consequently, they are leading their congregations away from the truth of the new covenant of grace and are placing them back under their own version of old covenant law. They are leading believers to do exactly what the writer of Hebrews warned them not to do, stray from the new covenant of grace.

By refusing to rest by faith in the finished work of Jesus, they are crucifying Jesus all over again with their religious works (Hebrews 6:6). In addition, they are trampling Jesus underfoot by treating his blood as unholy, and, in doing so, are insulting the Spirit of grace (Hebrews 10:29).

What is astonishing is these teachers and preachers are using Hebrews 6:6 and 10:26 to frighten believers into moral living, when the context of these verses is identifying people, like themselves, who have sinful, unbelieving, hardened hearts to the new covenant of grace.

It is no wonder so many believers wrestle with fear concerning the loss of their salvation, especially those with addictions. Living in fear of losing their salvation will eventually cause those who are battling with sin to give up and walk away from God because they view God as being angry with them rather than viewing God as being gracious and compassionate toward them.

Jesus Corrects The Distorted Views About God

Jesus, in correcting people's distorted views about God, resulting from the false teachings of the Pharisees, tells the story of the prodigal son (Luke 15:11-32). In this story, he reveals God is a Father who longs to be gracious to those in their sin. He is a Father who doesn't meet us with condemnation in our sin but compassion. He is a Father who doesn't meet us with anger but acceptance. He is a Father who doesn't meet us with frustration but forgiveness. He is a Father who doesn't meet us with a lecture but love.

God Is A Father Who Is Full Of Gracious Compassion

The revelation that God longs to be gracious and compassionate to you in your addiction will change your life. The revelation that God longs to pour his grace upon you will change your heart.

In reality, God has already poured his grace upon you through Jesus shedding his blood for all of your sins (Romans 5:15-17; Ephesians 1:6-8). In the new covenant, God is not waiting on you to cry out to him for grace. Rather, he simply wants you to receive through faith the grace he has already lavished upon you.

Once you place your faith in Jesus, you have eternal life. 1 John 5:11-13 says:

> *And this is the testimony: God has given us eternal life, and this life is in his Son. Whoever has the Son has life; whoever does not have the Son of God does not have life. I write these things to you who believe in the name of the Son of God so that you may know that you have eternal life.*

God Wants You To Know You Have Eternal Life

God wants you to know you have eternal life. He wants you to be at peace, no longer living in fear of losing your salvation. If you have placed your faith in Jesus, you have eternal life!

Will Some Use Grace As A License To Sin?

Is it possible some may use grace as a license to sin? Absolutely. Even though those who truly come to faith would never use grace as a license to sin, there are some false believers who may use grace in this way. In Jude 4, this is exactly what was happening. Some false believers were using grace as license to sin.

> *They turn the grace of our God into a license for immorality, and they deny our only Master and Lord, Jesus Christ.* (BSB)

Paul warned false believers, who were using grace as a license to sin, that they would not enter the kingdom of God (Galatians 5:19-21; Ephesians 5:5-7). In these verses, Paul's warning is not to believers struggling with or being tempted to sin, but his warning is to false believers who were mocking God by saying it was okay to use grace as a license to sin (Galatians 6:8).

Paul addressed those who asked if they could use grace as a license to sin in Romans 6 when he said:

> *What shall we say, then? Shall we go on sinning so that grace may increase? By no means! We are those who have died to sin; how can we live in it any longer?* (1-2)

> *What then? Shall we sin because we are not under the law but under grace? By no means!* (15)

We Will Battle Sin
We Will Battle Sinful Desires And Thoughts

Coming to faith in Jesus doesn't mean we will not battle sinful desires of the flesh and sinful thoughts in our minds. It doesn't mean we will not be tempted to sin. The truth is we will battle sin every day for the rest of our lives. This daily battle is a great sign that we are believers (Galatians 5:16-17).

I have talked with many believers, those with addictions and those who did not have addictions, who question if they really are believers, since they battle sinful desires daily. My encouragement to them is always that an unbeliever never battles sinful desires within him nor does he question if he is believer. Only a genuine believer battles sinful desires and questions the genuineness of his salvation. A false believer using grace as a license to sin never questions his salvation. This false believer is quite happy living a life of sin...no battle, no struggle at all, just making a mockery of grace.

We Have The Evil Desires Of Sin Within Us

Paul, who wrote we have died to sin, also wrote we have the evil desires of sin living in our flesh (Romans 6:12). He wrote that the Spirit is in conflict with our flesh and our flesh has cravings which long to be gratified (Galatians 5:17). Paul stated he, too, felt the weakness of battling sin and the inward burn of sin:

> *Who is weak, and I do not feel weak? Who is led into sin, and I do not inwardly burn?*

One of the reasons he was so dependent upon grace was because of his weaknesses and inward burn of sin (2 Corinthians 12:8-10). Had Paul not been established in grace, I am sure he would have given up and walked away from God, believing he had lost his salvation, or thinking he may not even be saved.

Believers who are not established in grace will live in torment as a result of their weakness in the flesh and their inward sinful burning. They will wonder if they really are believers in Jesus. Then, to add to that, a Bible teacher or preacher tries to convince them they can lose their salvation or attempts to get them saved again and again, with one altar call after another. If believers who are established in grace daily battle with sin, as did Paul, how much more difficult is the battle for believers who have never been established in grace?

He Was Convinced He Had Lost His Salvation

One of these believers not established in grace came into my office. His denominational preachers told him that if he sinned willfully (they were taking Hebrews 10:26 out of context), he would lose his salvation. He, like all of us, battled sinful desires within him. Sometimes, these sinful desires would burn within him. He constantly struggled with the ups and downs of not giving in to these desires. His struggles soon turned into an addiction. Because of his religious upbringing, he was convinced he had lost his salvation.

His wife invited to him to the church where I was the Pastor. She wanted him to hear about grace. He started coming to our services, where he learned about grace. The Holy Spirit began giving him the revelation of grace. Through the revelation of grace, liberation from years and years of religious bondage began happening in his heart and mind.

On the day he was in my office, he told me of the liberating effect grace had on his life. The reason, he said, he spiraled deeply into the darkness and despair of his addiction was because he was taught he could lose his salvation. This teaching produced hopelessness in his heart. Because he believed he lost his salvation due to his addiction, he reasoned "since I was going to hell, I might as well bust hell wide open."

This was a common phrase he heard over and over again from the leaders within his denomination. It became a part of his religious mindset. Consequently, he concluded, "Since I have lost my salvation and am going to hell, I might as well bust hell wide open by having as much fun on earth before I die." This drove him deeper into his addiction.

I am thankful his wife invited him to our church, where he heard the good news of God's grace. Understanding God's grace in all its truth rescued him from the pain of his addiction and restored him spiritually, mentally, emotionally, and relationally.

You Have Eternal Life

Please know, if you have come to faith in Jesus you have eternal life. You can't lose it. Ephesians 2:8-9 makes this crystal clear:

> *For it is by grace you have been saved, through faith—*
> *and this is not from yourselves, it is the gift of God— not*
> *by works, so that no one can boast.*

Your battle with your addiction will not cause you to lose your salvation nor is it a sign that you are not saved. You have been saved by grace through faith in Jesus. Your salvation is permanent. It is complete. It is forever. It is a gift from God to you.

He purchased this gift for you with the blood of Jesus. You have received it by faith. God wants you to enjoy his gift of salvation.

You can't enjoy it if you think you can lose it or if you think you may not have it because of your battle with addiction. You are saved by grace through faith. Be at peace in your salvation, knowing God will never take it from you.

Now that you understand grace, let's take a closer look at addiction.

PART TWO

A Closer Look At Addiction

14

The Process of Addiction

*There is a way that appears to be right,
but in the end, it leads to death.*
Proverbs 14:12

IN CHAPTER ONE, I asked the following question:

How do a people filled with such hope for the future, dreaming of what they would one day become, end up hurting themselves and the ones they love, living in misery and pain, and dreaming only of what could have been?

As I wrote in chapter one, people don't start off in life dreaming of being addicted to something then losing everything. Instead, they dream of doing something. They dream of becoming someone. Eventually, because of the addiction, they find themselves having nothing and all alone.

So how does this happen?

How Does An Addiction Begin?

An addiction doesn't just happen. There is a process to an addiction. Typically, the addiction begins in one of two ways: to experience pleasure or to escape pain.

Experiencing Pleasure

For many people, their addiction started casually. They were carrying no pain, no hurt, no emptiness, no loneliness, no fear, no anxiety, and no problems. They began spending time with a certain group of people or a certain person who eventually introduced them to the object of their addiction. They were told they would like it. They were encouraged to try it. So they did.

They tried it. They liked it. They were hooked. They were addicted. They did not realize this addiction, which at the time brought them great pleasure, would one day cause them great pain.

For others, they happened to find the object of their addiction in their home. Maybe it was something their parents or siblings had. They found it. They tried it. They liked it. They were hooked. They were addicted.

Escaping Pain

Though some begin their addiction to experience pleasure, others started their addiction to escape pain. There are many different types of pain people experience. However, they can be categorized mostly into these five areas: mental pain, emotional pain, relational pain, physical pain, and spiritual pain.

Mental pain has to do with our thoughts. Our thoughts become negative, discouraging, and pessimistic. Our thoughts are filled with fear and hopelessness. The source of these painful thoughts could have started in one's family. One could have grown up experiencing verbal abuse, hearing demeaning words over and over again.

Emotional pain is the feeling we have of being hurt deeply. Emotional pain, too, may originate from our thoughts. However, most of our emotional pain originates from difficult life experiences.

Relational pain has to do with hurtful relationships we have experienced. Relational pain could be the result of the relationship between a child and a parent, husband and wife, two friends, or one of many other relationships.

Physical pain is the pain our bodies feel. This pain could come from an injury or a surgery.

Finally, there is spiritual pain. This pain comes from disillusionment with God arising from a false belief about God. This disillusionment arises when we encounter problems in life that leave us wondering if there really is a God, and if there is, then why does he allow such pain into our lives. Disillusionment can also come from a spiritually abusive church or person.

Many people suffering from addiction have a combination of these different areas of pain. The addiction becomes their escape. For a moment, while under the influence of the addiction, they feel normal. They feel better. They find relief. They escape. But little did they know the addiction, which allowed them to escape pain, would become the continual source of great pain for a lifetime.

Maybe you can relate to one of these areas of pain. Maybe you can relate to a few areas of pain or to all the areas. Your life has been hard. You are hurting. To escape your pain, you turned to the object of your addiction.

Jesus Knows How You Feel
Jesus Experienced Pain

Jesus knows how you feel in your pain (Isaiah 53:3). You see, Jesus purposely endured the pain of life to its fullest degree. He experienced mental pain, emotional pain, relational pain, physical pain, and spiritual pain. Some say he even experienced the pain of sexual abuse as he was stripped naked of all his clothes, beaten, and then hung on the cross, fully exposed for all to see. He was verbally abused, physically abused, mentally abused, emotionally abused, and, at the hands of the Pharisees, spiritually abused. He even experienced the spiritual pain of being forsaken by God on the cross when the presence of God was withdrawn from him as he took all of the world's sin upon himself. In his pain, he cried out to God, *"My God, my God, why have you forsaken me?"*

The reason Jesus purposely experienced and endured the pain of life was so he would know what it is like to be you...to know your hurt...to know how you feel. He can sympathize with you in your weaknesses...in your sufferings.

Jesus' Heart Goes Out To You

For those whose origin of addiction was pain or pleasure, and for those whose origin of addiction was something not mentioned, Jesus' heart goes out to you. Jesus had a gracious and compassionate heart toward those hurting from sin, from life, from abuse, from pain, and from poor decisions. It was said about Jesus that he would not break a bruised reed nor would he blow out a smoldering wick.

> *A bruised reed he will not break, and a smoldering wick he will not snuff out, till he has brought justice through to victory.* (Matthew 12:20)

The bruised reed represented hurting people and the smoldering wick represented hopeless people.

Jesus daily interacted with people who were hurting and hopeless, people in need of his gracious compassion. I am sure many of these people had addictions. He spent so much time with them that the religious Pharisees labeled him "a friend of sinners" (Matthew 11:19). They criticized Jesus for welcoming them and eating with them. Yet their criticism was really a great compliment.

The Hurting Were Healed And The Hopeless Found Hope

Because of the time Jesus spent with these bruised reeds and smoldering wicks, and because of the gracious compassion flowing from his heart to theirs, their hurts were healed and their hopelessness turned into hope.

It is quite possible you find yourself both hurting and hopeless. Jesus loves you. With his gracious compassion, he wants to heal you and breathe hope into you. You can come to Jesus. You can talk with Jesus. He does not meet you with guilt and condemnation, but he meets you with grace and compassion.

15

The Pattern of Addiction

You were taught, with regard to your former way of life, to put off your old self, which is being corrupted by its deceitful desires; to be made new in the attitude of your minds; and to put on the new self, created to be like God in true righteousness and holiness.
Ephesians 4:22-24

EVERY ADDICTION HAS a pattern. Understanding the pattern of addiction will go a long way in helping you break free from your addiction. The pattern of addiction involves seven parts.

Part 1: The Reasons For Addictions
The reasons for addictions are typically to experience pleasure, because people are bored with life, or to escape pain, problems, and pressure, because people are burdened with life. Those seeking a cure to boredom with life through momentary pleasures eventually experience a lifetime of pain and problems, far-outweighing the pleasures. Those seeking to escape the pain, problems, and pressures in life actually add to their burdens.

Part 2: The Routine Of Addiction
Addictions have triggers. A trigger is what ignites the craving for the good feeling the addiction produces. For many suffering with addictions, the good feeling has long passed. Now the body and brain crave the addiction just to feel normal or to avoid feeling sick. This sickness is called withdrawals.   Withdrawals can be severely painful for those who do not give in to their cravings as they attempt to leave behind the life of addiction.

The Bible calls these cravings "cravings of the flesh." The cravings launch the pursuit of the addiction. The trigger, cravings, and pursuit working together become the routine. Here are eight common triggers.

Experiencing Adversity

Adversity is the pain, problems, and pressures of life. When some who are suffering with addiction experience adversity, their way to escape the negative feelings associated with adversity is through their addiction. It is their automatic escape. Yet, just like a ride at Disney World, it always lets them off where they got on...still facing the pain, problems, and pressures of life...only now, having added to them.

Having Anxiety

A major trigger for many people is anxiety. To calm themselves, they rely on different medications or alcohol. They become dependent upon medication or alcohol, or a combination of the two, to relax.

Many people suffer from social anxiety. Social anxiety is the uncomfortable feelings that come from being around people. It is important to know social anxiety is real.

Those with social anxiety believe there is something terribly wrong with them. Because they feel this way, they attempt, through their addiction, to escape the uncomfortable feelings associated with social anxiety, not realizing their addiction is creating even more anxiety in their lives.

A good way to deal with social anxiety is through acceptance. Having social anxiety doesn't make you a bad person. It doesn't mean you have a terrible life-altering condition that must be numbed through medication or alcohol. It doesn't define who you are. You are God's dearly loved child whom he has completely forgiven and totally accepted. You are not your condition. You are who your heavenly Father says you are...his beloved son or daughter.

By accepting your condition and knowing who you are to your heavenly Father, you can be free. You can be free from condemning yourself for having this condition and free to experience the joy of the positive side of social anxiety.

People with social anxiety have abilities where being alone is necessary. For example, some people who write have social anxiety. Writing requires hours and hours of being alone. It is in these hours of being alone the written product is formed and completed.

Many people who have artistic gifts such as music, drawing, painting, and designing have social anxiety. Yet it is social anxiety that grants them the alone time needed to allow their creative gift to be expressed and then bless the world.

Once I was talking to a dad whose son had social anxiety. From early childhood, he labeled his son as "my shy one." His son did not enjoy social settings but enjoyed being alone. Consequently, the dad assumed his son had a terrible problem that made him socially awkward, forcing him to withdraw from people into isolation.

To "fix this problem," he took his son to a psychiatrist. The psychiatrist put him on medication at a very young age to help the child avoid the symptoms of social anxiety, so he could function as a "normal person" in society. However, this medication didn't help. They tried altering the doses and, eventually, changing the medication, all in an attempt to "fix" the child. Nothing worked. Actually, he went deeper into his isolation, eventually into despair.

The child began to believe something was wrong with him. He believed he was "not like everyone else." He believed everyone else did great in social settings, yet he was different. He had issues. He had problems. This preoccupation with his "problem" consumed him and his dad. They tried to correct the problem, but to no avail...the problem only got worse.

In my conversation with the child's dad, he began to tell me his son, now in his twenties, was not doing well because he suffered so terribly from "shyness." He told me all they had done to try to help their son. I asked the dad what his child excelled in and what he enjoyed. He said his son loved to draw and paint. I explained to his dad that his shyness or social anxiety actually complimented his son's abilities, and it was quite possible his son never had a problem needing to be fixed, but he had abilities which his desire to be alone allowed to flourish. It was his son's desire to be alone that would allow him to discover and excel at his gift, possibly launching him into the career field for his life...a career he would enjoy and share with the world.

With this new insight into his son's personality, the dad began to see his son as not having a problem needing a solution, but as having potential needing to flourish. He then made the connection that for his son's potential to flourish, he needed to be alone. And, that if he was outgoing, his abilities would never be discovered and developed. With this insight, he saw his son's shyness as a gift that allowed his son to discover the God-given gift of drawing and painting.

In writing on social anxiety and addiction, I admit I am not a doctor, psychologist, or psychiatrist. I have never studied social anxiety in an academic or clinical setting. I would never recommend taking anyone off medication for any condition. That is a decision between a patient and his doctor.

Roy And Social Anxiety

Roy walked into my office to discuss his addiction. We soon discovered his addiction originated from social anxiety, which he perceived as a problem needing to be fixed. He concluded there must be something wrong with him, causing him to be uncomfortable in social settings. He was so uncomfortable when he was around people that he would sweat profusely. As I shared with him that he wasn't some type of odd person, needing to be "fixed," but was a person who had gifts, talents, and abilities that his "shyness" allowed him to flourish in, he began to sense a new freedom in his life. No longer did he define himself according to his social anxiety. Instead, he saw his desire to spend time alone as a gift from God, which allowed him to flourish in his giftedness.

Let's continue to examine triggers.

Being Alone

Being alone can be a trigger. When some people are alone, their cravings begin. As long as they are with people, they are okay. But as soon as they are alone, their flesh begins to strongly desire the object of the addiction.

Being Away

For some, their addiction started when they were away from home, such as on a business trip. This "new sense of freedom" from their perceived mundane life created an opportunity for excitement. In their pursuit of excitement to escape their "boring life," they discovered the object of their addiction. Once this discovery was made, they became addicted. The addiction then turned this new sense of freedom into a life of bondage.

Getting Angry

Anger is a trigger for many people. When they get angry, they turn to their addiction as a way to cope and to be calm. Many times, those with an addiction will create an argument with a loved one because they know it will give them an excuse for using. Then, they will blame their loved one for everything that happened.

Being Around Specific People

There are specific individuals or groups that a person with an addiction just can't be around. When around these individuals or groups, the pressure and urge to return to the addiction is strong.

Being At A Specific Place

When someone with an addiction is at a specific place, the

desire for the addiction kicks in. This place could be a certain neighborhood or street. It could even be at work. Many people have become addicted to certain drugs to give them the energy to perform their work duties.

Reaching A Specific Time

When the clock strikes a specific time, the craving of the addiction begins. The addiction knows what it wants when it wants it. So when a certain time of the day comes, the urge automatically arises within the body for the feeling that only the addiction can produce.

Anticipating An Event

Eagerly anticipating upcoming events is a strong trigger. The one with the addiction associates the addiction with the event. These events may include the weekend, a holiday, tailgating at a game, or social events, such as a wedding, party or family gathering. Events may be personal hobbies such as fishing, hunting, golfing, or playing softball. The one with an addiction finds it impossible to enjoy certain events unless he can experience the event along with the addiction.

By identifying triggers, those with addictions can begin to put together a plan to safely resist the addiction until the cravings pass. We will take a closer look at a plan in chapter eighteen.

Part 3: The Rush Of The Addiction

The rush of an addiction comes first from the anticipation of the addiction and then from participation in the addiction.

Anticipation Of The Addiction

The one suffering from addiction experiences an exciting rush of adrenalin in the anticipation of the addiction. The heart begins to beat rapidly and the chemicals in the brain begin to be released pleasurably. The excitement from this anticipation leads to the pursuit of the addiction, creating an even higher adrenalin rush.

Participation In The Addiction

Once those with an addiction have pursued and acquired the source of their addiction, they experience an even greater rush of adrenalin and pleasure when actually participating in their addiction.

Many people are addicted to the pleasurable rush of the addiction. Most addictions produce the same or similar feelings physically in the body and chemically in the brain. The one with a gambling or sexual addiction experiences the same or similar high as those with other addictions.

Part 4: The Regret Of The Addiction

When the rush of the addiction is over, regret from the addiction begins immediately, producing tremendous guilt and shame.

Guilt: Feeling Bad About What They Have Done

Once coming down off the high of the addiction, they begin to feel bad about what they have done. They regret their attitudes and actions towards others. They feel guilty. They say to themselves, others, and God, "I can't believe I did that. I promise I will never do it again." And they sincerely mean it but can't carry it out.

Shame: Feeling Bad About Who They Have Become

Soon guilt turns into shame. They hate themselves because of what they have done. They feel worthless. They feel like terrible people. They feel like failures. In their hearts and minds, they feel unloved and rejected by God and others, convinced they have let them down. Feeling this way, suicide becomes a real option. Then, to escape this feeling of suicide, some use again, but this time, not caring if they live or die.

The bait Satan used to lure them into the addiction, a promise to escape pain or experience pleasure, is now in total control of their lives, seeking to destroy them completely.

Part 5: Repentance From The Addiction

Because these feelings of guilt and shame are so strong, they make promises to themselves, God, and others. They promise to turn away from their addiction and to never go back. They make promises they will do better by practicing good deeds. These promises are sincere.

In making these promises, they truly believe their previous participation in their addiction was the last. By keeping these promises, they believe they will earn their way back into the "good graces" of God and their families. For a while, they do better. They feel better. The feel like they have earned their way back into God's and their family's love and acceptance. But eventually, they return to their addiction, creating even more guilt and shame.

This is what the people of Israel did in the Old Testament. They confessed to God their sins, told him how sorrowful they were, and promised God they would fully obey the law. Yet they failed again and again. So what did they do? They repented again and again, rededicating themselves to do better but then failing...again and again.

This was the repetitive cycle of the people of Israel as they lived under and rebelled to the law. It is also the repetitive cycle of many believers in Jesus. They promise God and others they will do better. But they fail. Again and again they fail. So they repent and dedicate themselves to doing better. This repetitive cycle continues for years, and for some, a lifetime.

The Biblical View Of Repentance
True Repentance Draws Us To God

The failure of these promises is rooted in a faulty

understanding of repentance. This faulty understanding of repentance is when a person attempts to avoid the anger, punishment, and rejection of God by telling God he is sorry, asking him for forgiveness, and trying to earn his way back into God's love and acceptance by promising to do better and practicing good deeds. This was the way the nation of Israel practiced repentance under the old covenant. However, it never worked.

True repentance is turning to God because he is loving, gracious, and compassionate toward us in our sin, longing to heal us with his forgiveness, kindness, and goodness. In turning to God, we are trusting him to change our lives.

True repentance is admitting we have tried and failed many times to change ourselves. We admit we are powerless to change, but the grace he freely offers in Jesus is powerful to change us. So rather than promising God we will do better, we turn to God and humbly admit we are helpless and hopeless to do better and our only help and hope is his grace. In this biblical view of repentance, we are drawn to the God of gracious compassion, believing he longs to heal and restore us.

God's Gracious Compassion Produces Repentance

This gracious God of compassion is who the prophets of the Old Testament told the people of Israel about. The prophets did warn the people about the consequences of continuing in their ways, but they also told the people about the graceful compassionate heart of God, longing to heal and restore them (2 Chronicles 2:9; Nehemiah 9:17, 31; Isaiah 30:18-19). The prophets understood it was God's gracious compassionate heart that would empower the humble, broken person to repent, or turn to God and be healed and restored...changed!

Religious Leaders Never Taught True Repentance

The true view of repentance was never taught by the religious leaders of Jesus' day. Instead, they propagated a false and destructive view of repentance.

The belief of those in Jesus' time, as well as some in our time, is repentance involves turning away from one's sin in order to avoid the punishment of an angry god. The religious leaders of Jesus' day never described God as being gracious and compassionate, longing for people to turn to him and experience his love, forgiveness, kindness, and goodness so he could heal and restore them (Romans 2:4).

God was presented falsely by these religious leaders. By not describing God as the God of gracious compassion to people in their sin, they completely misrepresented him.

Jesus Taught True Repentance

To confront the prideful, religious people of his day who continually distorted the character of God and to correct these distortions, Jesus told parables, or stories. One of the stories Jesus told was about a prodigal son who rebelled to his father's loving kindness. This son took all his inheritance at a young age, left home, and went to a faraway country where immorality was plentiful.

In this faraway country, the son experienced all the immoral pleasures available. Eventually, the son was penniless and hungry. When no one gave him any help, he worked on a farm taking care of pigs. His hunger became so intense that his only means of survival was to eat the pig slop.

Soon, becoming disgusted with himself and hopeless in his condition, he decided to return home to his father. He was convinced he would never be accepted back into his father's heart and home, unless he earned his way back.

In his mind, being accepted by his father and allowed back into his father's home would require repentance. So he devised a plan to earn his way back into his father's heart and home. His plan involved admitting to his father and to God he had sinned against them. And, since he was convinced he would never be allowed back into his father's heart or home unless he earned it, his plan included a promise to work hard on his father's farm as a hired servant. He was confident, by making and keeping his promise, his father would eventually open the door of his heart and home.

With his fully developed plan of repentance, he began his long journey home, fully prepared to meet the angry judgment of his father. As he journeyed closer to his home, he saw in the distance someone running toward him. Quite possibly, he thought someone was running toward him in anger...in hatred, with punishment in his heart.

As the fuzzy figure got closer to him, he noticed it was his father. He was probably thinking, "My father hates me and is going to tell me I am not allowed home. Good thing I have my repentance plan!"

So while his father was running toward him, he was rehearsing his plan. Then, the moment came, he was face to face with his father. Taking him by complete surprise, in total contrast to the response he expected from his father, the father in compassion reached out to his son and embraced him with grace.

While safe in the embrace of grace, the son admitted his sin to his dad. His father then did something his son was not expecting. The father did not allow his son to get another word out of his mouth about the rest of his plan. Instead, his father sent his servants to quickly bring the best robe and sandals for his son, a ring to place on his finger, and the fattened calf to be prepared for a festive party in celebration of his son's return.

Grace Produces True Repentance

There is so much in this story about how grace produces true repentance. We find in this story that God is not a god full of anger and judgment toward us in our sin, but he is a Father full of grace and compassion, wanting to bring healing and restoration to us. He is our Father who embraces us at our worst and quickly brings us his best. He doesn't punish us or make us learn our lesson by making us wait on his response to our sinful condition.

Through his gracious compassion, forgiveness, kindness, and goodness, we learn that God, our Father, moves swiftly to heal and restore us.

We also learn our Father doesn't make us work our way back into his heart. In view of our heavenly Father's grace, we discover it is impossible to earn our way into the heart of the one whose heart already loves and accepts us unconditionally. We discover there is no need for a religious plan of repentance based upon our efforts, because real repentance is produced by grace, leading to true life-change!

Dropping Our Religious Plans Of Repentance
Once we understand who God is...our gracious and compassionate Father who quickly runs to us in our sinful condition, we drop our religious plans of repentance and turn to him in real repentance, receiving his embrace of grace. His embrace of grace allows us to freely admit our sin and begin the process of being fully healed and restored.

Until a person understands the biblical view of repentance, they will repeat this pattern of addiction day after day...month after month after month...year after year after year.

Part 6: The Repetition Of The Addiction
Even though those trapped in their addictions promise to do better by practicing good deeds, they continuously repeat this pattern of addiction. Because they have a distorted view of God, they do not understand the biblical view of repentance.

Part 7: The Results From Addiction
Those suffering with addiction lose so much over the course of

their lives. Here is a sample of what an addiction causes people to lose:

> family, children, opportunities, ambition, time, interests, trust, jobs, money, integrity, reputation, character, health, dreams, hope, friends, relationships, possessions, personality, self-worth, standards, values, heart, weight, peace, joy, happiness, their mind

The last two losses are the loss of freedom...the prison yard, and the loss of life...the graveyard. Tragically, the one who started off in life dreaming of what he would be or do never thought he would end up in a prison yard or graveyard.

If you are reading this, there is one thing I know, you are not in a graveyard. You may have come close to death through overdoses or car accidents. You know you should be dead. But God, in has gracious compassion, has spared your life. He runs to you with grace. He reaches out to you with grace. He embraces you with grace. His grace is the pathway out of your addiction.

16

The Pathway Out Of Addiction

...the rising sun will come to us from heaven to shine on those living in darkness and in the shadow of death, to guide our feet into the path of peace.
Luke 1:79

YOUR ADDICTION HAS LED you into some very dark places physically, mentally, relationally, and emotionally. It has brought great pain into your life. It has made you feel worthless. It has made you feel hopeless. You carry around guilt and shame. You live in despair. Your pain and feelings of worthlessness and hopelessness, along with your guilt, shame, and despair, have kept you enslaved to your addiction, causing you to repeat the pattern of addiction over and over again. Now, shining brightly into the darkness of your addiction, is God's grace. His grace is healing your hurts, giving you hope, and bringing you peace. The Bible describes God's healing, hope, and peace.

> *"And you, my child, will be called a prophet of the Most High; for you will go on before the Lord to prepare the way for him, to give his people the knowledge of salvation through the forgiveness of their sins, because of the tender mercy of our God, by which the rising sun will come to us from heaven to shine on those living in darkness and in the shadow of death, to guide our feet into the path of peace."* (Luke 1:76-79)

Grace Shines Brightly In Your Darkness

Through Jesus, the grace of God shines like the morning sunrise in the darkness of your addition. It guides your feet onto the pathway of his peace. The pathway of his healing. The pathway of his hope. The pathway of his grace. Where once you saw no way out, his grace is the pathway out. This pathway is lit with God's love, forgiveness, and acceptance freely provided for you in Jesus. As you take steps of faith onto this pathway of grace, believing you are loved, forgiven, and accepted by God, you will be encouraged and strengthened.

> *May our Lord Jesus Christ himself and God our Father, who loved us and by his grace gave us eternal encouragement and good hope, encourage your hearts and strengthen you in every good deed and word.*
> (2 Thessalonians 2:16-17)

The light of his grace has now come to you in your darkness, proving God loves you and desires for you to hear the good news of his grace. The good news of his grace has come to you, not just as mere words, but as the mighty power of God. The Holy Spirit is deeply convincing you of the truths of God's grace. In the middle of your darkness...your suffering, you have welcomed the message of God's grace into your heart and mind. Joy is now bursting forth from within you!

Grace Is Working In You
Because you have accepted the message of his grace, it is now working in you. Others will see God's grace in you and hear about God's grace from you. 1 Thessalonians 1:4-7 and 2:13 describe what God is doing in your heart through grace.

> *For we know, brothers and sisters loved by God, that he has chosen you, because our gospel came to you not simply with words but also with power, with the Holy Spirit and deep conviction. You know how we lived among you for your sake. You became imitators of us and of the Lord, for you welcomed the message in the midst of severe suffering with the joy given by the Holy Spirit. And so you became a model to all the believers in*

Macedonia and Achaia. The Lord's message rang out from you not only in Macedonia and Achaia—your faith in God has become known everywhere. (1:4-7)

And we also thank God continually because, when you received the word of God, which you heard from us, you accepted it not as a human word, but as it actually is, the word of God, which is indeed at work in you who believe. (2:13)

Through this deep work of grace God is doing in your heart, you no longer see or define yourself as an addict or alcoholic but as a dearly loved, forgiven, and accepted child of God who has a problem with addiction or alcohol.

You Are Free To Be Transparent

This awareness of God's love, forgiveness, acceptance, and grace, allows you to be honest with God and others about your addiction. No longer fearing the rejection of God or others, you are free to be transparent. Through transparency, the transformation process begins.

1 Peter 5:6 says, *"God opposes the proud but gives grace to the humble."* Through humility, which allows you to experience God's grace, you freely admit your problem to yourself, to God, and to others.

For years you have attempted to hide your addiction in the darkness. Just like Adam and Eve in the Garden of Eden attempted to hide because of fear of rejection and punishment, you have attempted to hide.

Over and over again, you denied having an addiction. Over and over again, you lied to cover your addiction. When those who love you tried to talk to you about your problem, you became angry, sometimes blaming them or others for your addiction. By hiding, denying, lying, and blaming, you stayed in darkness, despair, and the destructive pattern of addiction. But now grace has come, shining the rays of God's love, forgiveness, and acceptance into your heart, providing a pathway out of your darkness.

Called Out Of Darkness Into God's Wonderful Light
1 Peter 2:9 says you have been called out of the darkness into God's wonderful light. Now you declare how great his grace is!

> *But you are a chosen people, a royal priesthood, a holy nation, God's special possession, that you may declare the praises of him who called you out of darkness into his wonderful light.*

On this journey into the wonderful light of God's grace, you have discovered you are powerless to get yourself out of the darkness of your addiction. But this powerlessness doesn't lead to depression. It actually leads to joy, because the awareness of your powerlessness leads you to the pathway of God's grace.

On this pathway of grace, you are discovering your life is not over. You are walking out of the darkness and despair of your addiction and into the light and love of God's grace, with a new sense of hope for the future.

17

A PICTURE OF A NEW LIFE

Now to him who is able to do immeasurably more than all we ask or imagine,
according to his power that is at work within us...
Ephesians 3:20

NOW THAT YOU ARE ON THE pathway of grace, you have hope for your life and future. God's grace, once shining brightly into your darkness and despair, is now showing you the way to a new life. You are picturing a life beyond your addiction made possible by the power of his grace. You are picturing a new life.

You Are Freed By Grace To Enjoy The Future
God is beginning to do something new in your heart. You feel it. You sense it. He is about to unleash the talents, gifts, and abilities he placed within you. The God-given dreams the addiction tried to steal are about to unfold in your life.

This picture of a new life you now have in your heart and mind excites you...empowers you...and energizes you! You no longer see yourself chained to the regret and guilt of your past, you now see yourself freed by grace to enjoy your future.

In a way, your future is your best friend. It offers a fresh start, freed by God's grace to hope again...to live again. Whereas your past was your worst enemy, reminding you of all you did wrong, begging you to live each day in regret of what you did yesterday, your future is your best friend, telling you to live each day rejoicing that God loves you and remembers your sins no more.

Released From Regret
Peter Was Released From Regret

The disciples had to go through regret before they received the revelation of God's grace. They all promised Jesus they would never abandon him. Peter promised Jesus that even if all the other disciples abandoned him, he never would. Yet, within hours of making these promises, all the disciples abandoned him. Peter even denied knowing him.

Peter deeply regretted what he did. He wept bitterly over it (Luke 22:62). He and the other disciples thought their lives were over. They returned to their previous way of life, fishing. Then unexpectedly, Jesus came walking on the shore. They didn't know it was him. He told them to throw their nets back into the water. Though they had been fishing all night and caught nothing, they cast their nets one more time. With one cast, they caught more fish than ever before. It was their biggest catch ever, their biggest payday ever!

Suddenly, their eyes were opened. They realized it was Jesus who told them to cast their nets into the water. Quickly, and with great excitement, they returned to shore, with Peter leading the way, swimming ahead of those coming to the shore in their boats. Upon arriving at the shore, Jesus had breakfast cooked for them. He spent time with them. He also spent private time with Peter, restoring Peter gracefully from the regret that gripped him. This graceful conversation allowed Peter to be released from his regrets (John 21).

Peter still had his ups and downs following this grace encounter with Jesus. Yet, over time, he continued to grow in grace, eventually becoming the leader of the disciples, spreading the good news about Jesus and writing two books.

In his last book, in the last verse, he writes the following:

But grow in the grace and knowledge of our Lord and Savior Jesus Christ. To him be glory both now and forever!
(2 Peter 3:18)

If anyone understood growing in grace, it was Peter. We all can relate to Peter. On one hand, we are aware of our sinfulness. On the other hand, in our pride, we see ourselves as more faithful than the others...more dependable. When we finally hit bottom, we see we are no different than anyone. Like everyone else, we need grace!

Then, as wave after wave of guilt and shame crash into our minds, Jesus comes walking to us on the shore of our lives. Gracefully, he calls out to us. Gracefully, he provides for us. Gracefully, he "cooks breakfast for us." Gracefully, he reminds us our lives are not over. With his grace, we are released from the regrets of our past and restored to a new life.

Paul Was Released From Regrets

Paul, too, battled with regrets. Remember, Paul was a religious terrorist. Violently, with children watching in horror, he stormed into synagogues and homes, dragging out fathers and mothers and husbands and wives, imprisoning them for their belief in Jesus. Some he even had put to death.

The memories of what he did would often haunt him. Whenever he was in towns and cities surrounding Jerusalem, I am sure he had flashbacks of his previous life as he saw fatherless children and husbandless wives because of what he had done. Messengers of Satan would come to him, reminding him of his past (2 Corinthians 12:7). Paul was tormented. Three times he asked Jesus to remove the painful thorn of regret, with which these messengers of Satan tormented him. In response, Jesus said to him, *"My grace is sufficient for you, for my power is made perfect in weakness"* (2 Corinthians 12:9).

Jesus knew grace was the ultimate healing from the memories haunting Paul. Jesus was saying to Paul:

> *Paul, I know you regret what you have done. I know the messengers of Satan torment you by reminding you daily about your regrets. I know these tormenting reminders weaken you with guilt, shame, and sadness. Paul, know*

that my grace shows up best when you are at your worst. My grace is the power you need to be released from your regrets. I love you. I died for you. I have forgiven you. Forgive yourself. Live daily in my grace. When those tormenting messengers are sent by Satan to remind you of your guilt, remember my grace. My grace is more powerful than Satan's messengers. My grace is more powerful than your guilt.

Paul's response to Jesus' reply of grace was to delight in his own weaknesses, because in his weaknesses, the grace of Jesus began working in his heart. Paul, in no way, delighted in what he had done, but he did delight in God's grace, which freed him from what he had done. Through grace, Paul was able to forget what was behind and move forward in his new life (Philippians 3:13-14), confident in Jesus' love for him (Galatians 2:20).

You Can Be Released From Regrets

You have your regrets, too, bad things you wish you would not have done...good things you wish you would have done. You picture them over and over again in your mind. You are tormented by these regrets. Because of grace, these regrets have not ruined your life. You can forget the past and move forward into your future. Hear Jesus saying to you, *"My grace is sufficient for you. I love you. I died for you. I have forgiven you. Forgive yourself."*

When you receive God's grace in your regrets, you will begin to be released from them. A picture of a new life will emerge in your mind. Actually, this is happening to you right now as you receive the revelation of God's grace, you are picturing a new life!

You Are A New Person With A New Identity

God's grace not only produces a new life, but it also creates a new person with a new identity. Ephesians 2:10. *"For we are his workmanship, created in Christ Jesus for good works, which God prepared before that we would walk in them"* (World English Bible). You are a person who has been created in Christ Jesus through his grace.

You have a new identity in Christ. Your identity is not defined by your past, your failures, your behaviors, or your addiction. Your identity is determined by what Jesus has done for you. You are a loved, forgiven, righteous, and accepted child of God. You are at peace with God, under no condemnation, and freed from the law. Jesus now lives in you. You call God *"Abba (Dad, Papa) Father."*

You are a person God has created for good works. Before you were ever born, not only did God know you would need grace because of your addiction, but he prepared good works for you. So your salvation, identification, and your destination are all by his grace.

Think Differently About Yourself

For you to walk in the good works God has prepared for you, you must think differently (Romans 12:1-4). Romans 12:2 says, *"...be transformed by the renewing of your mind."* Ephesians 4:23 says, *"be made new in the attitude of your mind."* Ephesians 4:24 says, *"put on the new self."*

You are not who you used to be. You have a new identity. You have a new life. God has prepared good works for you to walk in. This is the new self.

As you begin to think differently about yourself, you will have opportunities to make new decisions. Your decisions will determine the direction of your life. Your decisions will be fueled by knowing you are a new person with a new identity and a new life.

Remember Who You Are And Where You Are Going

As you make these decisions, do not be surprised when the sinful desires of the flesh come against you and try to deceive you into making the wrong decisions (Romans 6:12; Ephesians 2:3, 4:22), so that you go back to your former way of life, reaping its destruction. When the sinful desires of the flesh come against you, seeking to destroy you through deception, remember who you are...a new person with a new identity and a new life!

Your Harvest Will Come
Also, as you make decisions, know that you will not see immediate results. Making decisions is like a farmer planting seeds in his garden. He has a beautiful picture in his mind of his harvest. This picture motivates him. Every day he wakes up, gets up, and shows up to work in his garden, not seeing immediate results. But eventually, as he continues to wake up, get up, show up, and work hard, he will see a harvest. Not only will he benefit from his harvest, but people in his family and community will too.

Wake Up, Look Up, Get Up, And Show Up Every Day
You have a beautiful picture in your mind of a harvest in your life. That future will not just happen. Empowered by God's grace, wake up every day, look up to God (this is a figure of speech since he lives in your heart), get up from bed, show up to work, or wherever you need to be that day, work hard, and then go home and do it again the next day...and the next day...and the next day. And then one day, you will reap a harvest in your life that not only benefits you but also those in your family and community.

Never Give Up
As you wake up, look up, get up, show up, and work hard every day, and then go home and do it again the next day, there will be some challenges to overcome. There will be boring days. There will be difficult days. But never give up. If you keep making the right decisions and working hard every day, you will reap a harvest. Trust the process and you will reap a harvest.

Your Daily Schedule And Decisions
It is so important to understand the power of your daily schedule and decisions. Never take a day off, unless it is a scheduled day. Never wake up and say, "Well, I am tired today. I do not feel like getting up. I think I will take the day off." Every day get up, no matter how you feel, and make the right decisions all day.

The book of Proverbs is filled with wisdom for making great daily decisions. I highly recommend you read the book of Proverbs daily, not out of legalistic, religious obligation, but to provide you with the information and motivation to make the right decisions each day.

Little Compromises Cause Big Problems
One of my favorite sections in Proverbs is 24:31-34. It speaks about a man who began making little compromises in his daily decisions. These small compromises eventually produced disastrous results in his life. At first, he thought these little compromises were no big deal. Yet all these little compromises eventually added up to create destruction in his life.

Never underestimate the importance and impact of daily decisions on your life...even the little decisions. These little decisions, which may seem insignificant at the time, will add up over time, impacting your life either positively or negatively. Because of the power of decisions, keep making the right decisions every day, no matter how you feel and no matter how small the decision may seem.

Stay In The Correct Lane
The road into a place I used to work split into two separate lanes for a very moment and then came back into one road. It was easier to take the lane that was for the oncoming traffic than it was to stay in the correct lane. Because I valued the importance and impact of my daily decisions, no matter how insignificant they seemed, I chose to stay in the correct lane. I never want to allow

myself to get into the habit of letting an exception occur, no matter how I feel or how small it seems. I always want to act as if every decision I make is very important, no matter how unimportant it may seem. By doing this, I am establishing the habit of making good decisions.

Every Decision Matters, Every Day Matters

I want to encourage you to never let an exception occur in your decisions. Every decision matters. Every day matters. One wrong decision can undo a thousand right decisions, bringing devastating consequences. By valuing every decision every day of your life, you will avoid disastrous results and build toward a great future. You will establish habit patterns consistent with your new identity as God's loved, forgiven, and accepted child. Your life will move in the direction of the picture in your heart and mind...the picture of a new life!

18

A Plan For Living Beyond Your Addiction

The plans of the diligent lead to profit,
just as surely as haste leads to poverty.
Proverbs 21:5

HAVING A PLAN is vital to living beyond your addiction and experiencing a new life. A plan is a pre-determined set of decisions to be made every day that will lead you in a specific direction and guide you to your ultimate destination.

Your ultimate destination is the picture in your heart and mind of a new life. You are moving toward becoming a better husband, wife, dad, mother, son, daughter, brother, sister, person, etc...You are moving toward becoming everything God created you to be!

The Plans Of The Diligent

Proverbs 21:5 says, *"The plans of the diligent lead to profit just as surely as haste leads to poverty."* The diligent are the ones who every day follow their plan no matter how they may feel. They never make an excuse for not following their plan, nor do they let an exception occur. They understand if they follow their plan every day, no excuses and no exceptions, then one day they will see amazing results and will reap an abundance of rewards.

In this verse, we see that haste leads to poverty. Haste is failure to follow the plan because of a poor approach. Those who approach their plan hastily have a mindset that is not committed to following the plan. They make excuses and let exceptions occur. They may say things like:

No one will see.

It doesn't matter.

It's no big deal.

It's not hurting anyone.

One time will not hurt.

It will feel good.

I deserve it.

Because they have a poor approach to their plan, they eventually find themselves in poverty...the loss of all they value in their lives.

Two Approaches To A Plan
The difference between a person who experiences profit and one who experiences poverty is each one's approach to their plan. One person is wholeheartedly committed to fulfilling the plan no matter what happens and no matter how he feels. The other is half-heartedly committed to the plan and will easily deviate from the plan if he doesn't feel like doing something in the plan or if there are difficulties to overcome. The person with a wholehearted commitment knows if he perseveres in his plan, he will reap a harvest.

Perseverance is sticking with what you start no matter how you may feel and no matter how great the struggle because you know you will see amazing results and reap an abundance of rewards if you do not give up.

The Value Of Perseverance
Jesus talked about the necessity of perseverance if one is to reap a harvest.

But the seed on good soil stands for those with a noble and good heart, who hear the word, retain it, and by persevering produce a crop. (Luke 8:15)

So to live beyond your addiction, becoming the person you want to be, it is vital to have a plan and to value perseverance. Let's now look at a plan that will help you live beyond your addiction and experience a new life.

Refuse To Blame Others
Placing blame on others is a part of the human nature. After eating fruit from the tree in the garden, Eve placed blame on the Serpent, and Adam placed blame on Eve and God.

One of the first responses by those with an addiction is to deflect attention away from themselves, as did Adam and Eve, by placing blame for the addiction on another person. By placing blame on others, people avoid admitting they have a problem and avoid accepting responsibility for their own decisions. Consequently, they stay stuck in their addiction, causing further hurt and pain in their lives and in the lives of those who love them. Until people refuse to stop blaming others for their addiction, they can never recover from their addiction.

Admit You Have A Problem
No More Hiding

The first step necessary to living beyond your addiction is to admit to God, others, and yourself that you have a problem. Most people with an addiction try to hide it from others. However, the longer they hide their addiction, the longer they will hurt themselves and others. The first step to being set free from an addiction is to no longer keep it a secret.

The strength of the addiction is in keeping it a secret. The power of an addiction is keeping it private. By admitting your addiction to yourself, God, and others, the strength of the addiction begins to weaken and the power of the addiction begins to be broken.

Hiding from God and others is what Adam and Eve did after they sinned. We tend to do the same thing when we do wrong. We hide. We cover up. We lie. We deny.

Why do people hide their addiction in secrecy and privacy? The answer...shame and fear. Adam and Eve hid from God because they were ashamed and afraid. These are the same reasons people hide their addiction. They are ashamed of what they have done. Through hiding, they seek to avoid embarrassment and humiliation. They are afraid because of what they have done. They are afraid of rejection. They are afraid of abandonment. They are afraid of the consequences.

Established In God's Love

Shame and fear are produced in the hearts of those who are not established in God's love. Since they are not established in God's love, they keep their addiction a secret. Satan's goal is to keep those with an addiction living in fear because he knows the strength of an addiction is secrecy. However, by being established in God's great love, those with an addiction can freely admit their addiction to God because they are assured of his unconditional love for them. Because they are confident in God's love, they are free to admit their addiction to themselves and others. So regardless of how others respond to your addiction, and regardless of the consequences, you can rely on God's love (1 John 4:16).

Accept Your Past

There is not one thing you can do in the present to undo what you have done in the past or undo what was done to you. So don't spend the rest of your life wishing you could undo what you have done or undo what others have done. Instead, accept your past. Please know acceptance doesn't mean approval. Acceptance is not minimizing what was done. Acceptance is admitting what was done and choosing to move forward in your life by not dwelling on it or defining yourself by it.

The Power And Peace Of Acceptance

There is power and peace in acceptance. Acceptance empowers you to move on and enables you to have peace. Many people in the Bible had to accept their past in order to have the power and peace necessary for moving into the future. Peter had to accept his past. Paul had to accept his past. Another person who accepted his past was Joseph.

Joseph Accepted His Past

Joseph was abused, attacked, and abandoned by his brothers. To them, he was no more than a piece of property, having no value as a person. He was sold as a slave, eventually becoming a slave in the home of Potiphar.

While in Potiphar's home, Potiphar's wife daily tried to persuade Joseph to have a sexual relationship with her. Yet he refused. She eventually accused him of raping her. He was sentenced to prison for a crime he did not commit and was locked up in prison with chains around his neck, hands, and feet in the darkest, dirtiest part of the prison (Psalm 105:18).

Despite his past experiences, there was something remarkable about Joseph. He refused to become a bitter person. Rather than holding on to grudges, he held out grace. Rather than living in frustration over what happened to him, he lived by giving forgiveness to those who hurt him. Rather than becoming a victim in his circumstances, he rose victoriously from his circumstances, being appointed to the second highest position in all of Egypt by Pharaoh himself.

Judas Couldn't Accept His Past

Unlike Peter, Paul, and Joseph, who accepted their pasts, there was one who could not accept what he had done...Judas. Judas experienced tremendous shame and guilt because he betrayed Jesus. His shame and guilt drove him to commit suicide.

Suicide is not about death. Suicide is about escaping the agonizing pain inside a person. Judas' suicide was not about taking his life...it was about killing his pain. He could not live with the pain of his shame and guilt for another moment. So he killed the pain by taking his life.

What Judas didn't know was that God's grace was available for him. God's grace is not reserved for those whose sins are not as bad as others' sins. God's grace is readily available to all and is simply received by faith.

Just as Satan convinced Judas to take his life, he wants to convince you to take your life. Under his influence, but not realizing it, you have fantasized about suicide. He may have even glamorized it in your mind. The reason he wants you to take your life is because he knows God has a plan and purpose for your life. And if he can get you to take your life, he knows you will never experience God's plan and purpose.

If you have contemplated suicide to escape the pain of your addiction, please know you are not alone. This is a common feeling of many who battle addiction. I know you think you and your family would be better off if you took your life, but that is a satanic lie.

Suicide will prevent you from experiencing God's plan for your life and prevent others from experiencing the good things that will come into their lives through you. Additionally, it will leave your family devastated. It will be a terrible pain they live with for the rest of their lives. Even though you think by taking your life you will relieve your family of pain, it will be just the opposite. It will be the greatest pain in their lives. It will be a pain they will live with every day. It will be an unending pain. Taking your life will bring more pain into their lives than the addiction ever did.

The best, most loving decision you can make for your family...for your wife, children, mother, father, brothers, and sisters is to admit you have a problem, ask for help, and then go to where the help is. That may be a recovery center or recovery group. By going to a recovery center or group, you will get your life back, and your family will get you back. It will be a decision you will be glad you made.

Escape Your Pain Through Grace

Maybe you can relate to Peter, Paul, Joseph, or even Judas. Your past is painful. But you do not have to kill the pain by taking your life. You can begin to escape the pain, by receiving God's grace and giving God's grace.

There is nothing you can do to change your past. But through God's grace, you do not have to be chained to it. Through his grace, you can now accept your past and move forward in peace.

Forgive Yourself And Others

Part of accepting your past is experiencing God's forgiveness, forgiving yourself, and forgiving others. Through God's grace, you have been forgiven. Through God's grace, you can forgive yourself. And through God's grace, you can forgive others.

In previous chapters, I wrote about experiencing God's forgiveness and forgiving yourself, but I have written very little about forgiving others.

Joseph Gave Grace Away

Joseph could have died a bitter slave in Egypt, not only chained up physically, but bound up mentally and emotionally with anger and bitterness. Yet by choosing to hold out grace, rather than holding onto a grudge, he was released from the anger and bitterness that could have kept him enslaved. Because of grace, he moved forward into a brighter future and became a better person.

Graciously Giving Away Grace
> Ephesians 4:31-32 says:

> *"And do not grieve the Holy Spirit of God, with whom you were sealed for the day of redemption. Get rid of all bitterness, rage and anger, brawling and slander, along with every form of malice. Be kind and compassionate to one another, forgiving each other, just as in Christ God forgave you."*

These verses teach us the way to get rid of bitterness, rage, anger, brawling, and slander is by giving away grace. The original Greek word for forgiving in this verse is *charizomai*. It comes from the Greek word for grace which is *charis*. *Charizomai* means to graciously give away God's grace.

Preceding Ephesians 4:31-32, Paul, the author of Ephesians, wrote extensively on God's grace. He wrote how God lavished his grace upon us by forgiving our sins (Ephesians 1:3-8). and that through God's grace we have been saved (Ephesians 2:1-10). He also wrote that in the coming ages we will enjoy his grace every day (Ephesians 2:7).

Now Paul is encouraging us to give away the grace God has so freely given to us. Paul is encouraging us to graciously give away God's grace to those who have hurt us...who have wronged us...who have abused us...accused us...attacked us...abandoned us. He tells us that by giving away God's grace, we will free ourselves from the anger and bitterness holding us hostage inside our hearts and minds.

This verse says not to "grieve the Holy Spirit." Grieving the Holy Spirit has been greatly misinterpreted by Bible teachers. Many teach that to grieve the Holy Spirit is to make him mad or to "quench his Spirit." But this is not the context.

The word grieve is deeply rooted in the word love. Only love grieves. Grieve means to hurt deeply from a heart of love because of a loss. The Holy Spirit, as we learned in chapter eleven, desires to give us the revelation of God's love and grace freely given to us in Jesus and to establish us in the love of Christ in our inner being. Because we are so loved by the Holy Spirit, he grieves when we do not give away God's grace. He grieves for us because he knows by holding on to grace for ourselves, and not giving it away to others, we will stay imprisoned in our own cell of bitterness and anger, hurting ourselves and others. He wants to see us freed from the prison of what others have done to us and from the prison of our own anger and bitterness. We are freed by giving grace away.

Stephen Gave Grace Away
Giving grace away is what Stephen did just before he died. Stephen was a man full of grace (Acts 6:8). He had been arrested by the religious leaders. They were so furious with Stephen that they violently killed him.

Ironically, giving approval of his death, was Paul...yes Paul...the one who became the great communicator of grace, but was at one time the great terrorist of a religion. Before Paul's encounter with the grace of Jesus, he arrested many, having some put to death. One of these he had put to death was Stephen.

Just before Stephen's final breath, he fell to his knees and cried out, "*Lord, do not hold this sin against them*" (Acts 7:60). Stephen, like Joseph, could have died a bitter person. But, like Joseph, rather than holding onto a grudge, he held out grace. One of the people he held out grace to was Paul. We can't help but think of the impact Stephen's act of grace had on Paul's life.

Jesus Gave Grace Away
One more person who held out grace, rather than holding onto a grudge, was Jesus. He was rejected, hit, whipped, mocked,

abused, and accused. Yet, as he breathed his last few breaths, he said, *"Father, forgive them, for they do not know what they are doing"* (Luke 23:34).

Joseph, Stephen, and Jesus each provide an example of giving away grace to those who have hurt us. Each could have died a very bitter person. But rather than holding onto a grudge, they held out grace.

For you to move forward into a new life, choose to let go of the grudge you have been holding. Choose to give away God's grace.

Let's continue to look at a plan to help you break free from your addiction.

Consistently Attend A Recovery Group
Attending a recovery group is essential to breaking free from addiction and living a new life. You have tried to defeat your addiction by yourself, but it hasn't worked. This is because trying to defeat your addiction alone is like playing the best professional basketball player one-on-one in basketball. He will beat you every time. However, if you get some good basketball players on your team, the chances of beating him increases dramatically.

In the same way, your addiction, one-on-one, will beat you every time. You need a team...a team of people who help you do what you can't do alone...defeat your addiction. This is what a recovery group is...a team of people who help you do what you can't do alone.

Once you find a group, whether it is *Celebrate Recovery*, *re:generation*, AA, NA, SA or another group in your community or church, go every time the group meets.

In a recovery group, you will discover you are not alone, and there are many others with similar experiences. These groups provide opportunities to connect and talk with others, as well as provide recovery tools to help you. Through recovery groups, you will find mentors who will be there to help you.

Two very good recovery programs are *Celebrate Recovery* and *re:generation*. You can google each of these to find a group close to you. Once you find a group, whether it is *Celebrate Recovery*, *re:generation*, AA, NA, SA or another group in your community or church, go every time the group meets.

Resist making a judgment on your group the first several times you attend. This is because your first meetings will be awkward. You will be nervous. You will not know anyone. But if you keep going, you will build friendships with others who will support you in your recovery journey. Eventually, you will be able to help others who are just beginning their journeys.

I highly recommend you attend several different recovery groups in your area each week. For example, in my home town, there are four *Celebrate Recovery* groups. Each group meets on a different day. I strongly encourage those I counsel to attend all four groups, especially early in your recovery. There are also other recovery groups such as *The Most Excellence Way*. The more groups you attend weekly, the better off you will be.

As you remain committed to consistently attending your groups, never letting an exception occur or making an excuse to miss a group, one day you will see amazing results and reap the abundance of rewards. Remember, trust the process.

Sexual Addiction
Probably, the most shame-based addiction is sexual addiction. It is much easier to admit having a drug or alcohol addiction than it is to admit having a sexual addiction. Consequently, many people stay stuck in this addiction. However, there is hope. There are programs available for those battling this addiction. Here are several programs designed to help people with sexual addictions.

Heart to Heart Counseling: www.drdougweiss.com - Dr. Weiss also has resources on his other website, www.sexaddict.com.

Covenant Eyes: www.covenanteyes.com
Faithful and True: www.faithfulandtrue.com
Pure Heart Ministries: www.pureheartministries.net
Blazing Grace: www.blazinggrace.org

Healing Your Marriage When Trust Is Broken (Book): By Cindy Beall – This book is for wives of husbands with a sexual addiction.

If you have a sexual addiction, reach out for help. Your feelings will scream at you telling you to avoid embarrassment by staying silent. Yet you will only break free by breaking the silence. Remember, you are fully and forever loved, accepted, and forgiven by God. You are righteous before him, under no condemnation from him, and at peace with him. He doesn't look at you in disgust. He delights in you as his son or daughter. He will be with you when you break the silence. He will be with you to help you break free from your addiction. Others may reject you, but God never will.

Call Your Recovery Partner Daily
After you get involved in a support and recovery group, be sure to find a recovery partner or a mentor in your group. If you have trouble finding a mentor with whom you have chemistry, keep looking, eventually you will find someone with whom you connect and who will be of great value to you.

A recovery partner is someone committed to helping you break free from your addiction. It is someone you can meet with separately from the group, talk with, and learn from, since they have walked your road. You can be open and honest with your partner, knowing you will not be judged.

Call Your Sponsor Daily
You will want to call your sponsor or mentor every day for encouragement. The reason you will need to call him every day is

because one day, the urge to step back into your addiction will surface. At this point, you will need to call your partner immediately. If you have not been calling your partner daily, then, when you need him the most, you will not call. The phone will feel like a million pounds! But, if you have been calling your partner every day, then the phone will not feel so heavy, and by calling, the urge to step back into your addiction will be stopped.

Have Several People You Call Daily

I highly recommend having several people who you call daily, not just one. This allows you to develop a team of people who can help you reach your goal of living beyond your addiction. You have tried in isolation to defeat your addiction in the past. But now, you are forming a team. This team will not only be people you can reach out to, but also ensures someone will be available for you to talk with when the urge to step back into your addiction presents itself.

Be Open And Honest
Break Free By Breaking Your Silence

Openness and honesty are two of the keys to continued recovery. Decide not to keep any thought or action a secret. Remember, the strength of an addiction is a secret. By breaking your silence, you can break free. Find someone with whom you can share your thoughts and actions with consistently. The longer you keep a thought or action a secret, the stronger it gets. To release the strength of a secret, tell someone. The addiction will be weakened simply by telling someone.

Resist Silence And Secrets

You will be tempted not to tell others what is going on in your heart and mind. This is because you will be afraid of what they will think of you, certain they will be mad at you, and convinced you have disappointed them.

ᴐu may think they now believe you have overcome your
ᴀᴜᴅ n and all is well. Since you do not want them to think
badly about you, be angry with you, or be disappointed with you,
you stay silent and secretive. Resist silence and secrets. Find
several people in your life whom you are in touch with daily that
you tell every thought, desire, and action. Through openness and
honesty, you will be empowered to escape the bondage of your
addiction and to live in the freedom of new life.

Get Involved In A Grace-Based Church
There are many grace-based churches being established all
around the world. By being involved in a grace-based church, you
will meet a great group of people who you can grow with in God's
grace. The church will have different groups you can join and
areas you can serve. They will offer conferences and retreats. I
highly recommend you become a part of the men's ministry or
women's ministry. Join a small group. Your involvement in a
grace-based church will impact your life tremendously, helping
you live beyond your addiction.

Focus On Growing
As you focus on growing as a person, you will get better. Get
around people who are growing. Find a good Christian book to
read. Authors such as John Maxwell, Andrew Farley, Bob
Christopher, Bob George, and Matt McMillen have all written very
good books. I have also written another book called *The Story of
Grace*. You will find many resources on my website,
www.simplygrace.info, that are available for your personal
growth.

Exercise Weekly
Exercise is vital to recovery. Addictions harm the body and brain.
By exercising, you can begin reversing the effects of the addiction.
Exercise brings healing not only to the body but also to the brain.

You will feel good physically and mentally when you exercise. Find a local fitness center to attend. If necessary, ask the fitness trainer to help you with a fitness plan.

Place A Rubber Band On Your Wrist

Your brain and body experience pleasure through the addiction. Each has become addicted to the high the addition produces. They automatically associate the addiction with pleasure. By popping the rubber band each time you are tempted, your brain and body begin to associate the addiction with pain rather than pleasure. As you pop your wrist over and over each time you are tempted, your cravings will begin to decrease because your brain and body will no longer crave what brings pain.

Invest Time In A 90 Day Spiritual Development Plan

A spiritual development plan is one that focuses completely on your spiritual growth. A plan I recommend for those in addiction is a *90 Day Spiritual Development Plan,* where a person for 90 days develops spiritually by reading a daily writing such as *Living Free In Christ* by Neil Anderson. Soon, I will have an *Addicted To Grace 90 Day Spiritual Development Plan.*

I highly recommend Matt McMillen. Through grace, Matt has overcome alcoholism. He has written several books and has a daily email devotional. You can purchase his books or sign up for his daily devotionals at www.mattmcmillenministries.com.

You may enjoy listening to a podcast of your favorite Bible teacher or speaker. I recommend *Growing In Grace* by Mike Kapler and Joel Brueseke, *The Grace Café Podcast*, *The Fields Brothers Show*, *The UNSunday Show*, *Basic Gospel*, and *Andrew Farley*. On my website (simplygrace.info), I have a list of grace-based Bible teachers and writers who you would enjoy.

You may also get daily teachings sent directly to your email from Neil Anderson (www.ficm.org), Andrew Farley (www.andrewfarley.org), or Bob Christopher (basicgospel.net).

My website has hundreds of articles on grace I have written (www.simplygrace.info). By investing in this *90 Day Spiritual Development Plan*, you will grow spiritually as you renew your heart and mind.

If you miss a day, don't worry about it. Don't let others put you under their religious law that says you must have a devotion or quiet time every day or read your Bible and pray every day. If would like to have a quiet time or read the Bible and pray daily, that is your decision. God doesn't have that expectation. He wants a relationship with you, not a performance. Enjoy your spiritual journey of grace. Don't let others turn it into spiritual bondage.

Unleash Your God-Given Gifts, Talents, And Abilities

God knit you together with gifts, talents, and abilities that Satan has tried to steal through the deception of your addiction. The addiction, once promising great pleasure, has produced great pain. Be encouraged! Because of God's grace, your life is not over. You have not ruined your life. God wants you to enjoy life again by experiencing the abundant life that is yours through the grace Jesus brings.

There are God-given talents, abilities, and dreams within you waiting to be unleashed. Through the power of his grace, God will fulfill his plan for your life. Do not let Satan's addiction rob you of one more second of the life you were created to live!

Develop A New Set Of Friends

In order to stay away from your old life, you must stay away from your old friends. To step forward into your new life, you must develop a new set of friends. The Bible says, "*Whoever walks with the wise grows wise, but a companion of fools suffer harm*" (Proverbs 13:20).

The principle of this verse is that whoever we spend the most time with is who we become the most like. Therefore, it is vital for you to consistently get around people who are growing in their relationship with God and to stay away from those who will entice you back into your addiction.

This will be difficult because you will have to say "No" to your old friends. Know, however, that saying "No" to your old friends is saying "Yes" to those who love you and "Yes" to a new life.

Take The 30 Day Christian Music Challenge

Music is powerful. It influences our minds, emotions, desires, and decisions. For some, their addiction feeds on music. Depending on what type of music we listen to, we will either feed our flesh or Spirit. By listening to Christian music, we feed our Spirit and renew our minds. It helps create in us healthy emotions and desires and empowers us to make good decisions.

The Power Of Christian Music

One day I was listening to K-Love. K-Love is a Christian radio station that seeks to impact the lives of people by encouraging them to take their *30 Day Challenge* of listening to only Christian music for thirty straight days.

While I was listening to K-Love, someone who had taken their *30 Day Challenge* called the station. This person was in the recovery process from an addiction. He said he had an argument with his wife and was about to return to his addiction. When he started his car, his radio was tuned to K-Love because he had taken the *30 Day Challenge*. As he listened to the songs K-Love was playing, peace came into his heart and mind. He decided not to return to his addiction. Instead, he returned home to his wife.

I want to encourage you to take K-Love's *30 Day Challenge*. Listen to only Christian music for 30 days, and watch how your heart and mind are renewed.

Read Ten Pages Of An Uplifting Book Each Day

In his book, *The Slight Edge*, Jeff Olson recommends that those who want to experience a changed life read ten pages of an uplifting book each day. He says by reading ten pages each day, you will read several books in one year, which will have a great impact on your life. I suggest you start with Jeff's book, *The Slight Edge*.

In his book, he shares the principles which took him from living on the streets in Florida, having nothing, to becoming a millionaire and speaking to Fortune 500 Companies. You will be inspired by his book!

Be Aware Of Your Triggers
A trigger is anything that creates an urge tempting you to return to your addiction. By being aware of your triggers, you will not be surprised when these urges are triggered and temptations come, but you will be prepared to respond to them in a healthy way.

Here is a list a common triggers.

- *When you experience adversity.*

- *When you are alone.*

- *When you are away.*

- *When you have anxiety.*

- *When you are angry.*

- *When you are around a person.*

- *When you are affected by someone else's attitude or actions.*

- *When you are at a certain place.*

- *When you associate your addiction with a hobby such as hunting, fishing, softball, or golfing.*
- *When you anticipate a certain event such as the weekend, a holiday, game, or social event, or when you celebrate an event, game, etc...*

Conquer Your Cravings
What is a craving? A craving is an intense urge of the body yearning to be satisfied by returning to your addiction.

Here are 12 ways to not let your cravings control you.

1. Be honest with God about the craving you are having. God is not sitting in judgment on you because of your craving, but he is looking upon you with love. He is with you, loves you, and wants to hear from you.

2. Pop your rubber band.

3. Call your mentor, sponsor, and team members immediately. Be transparent with them about the temptation you are having.

4. Tell yourself:

- *This is not my craving, but the craving of my flesh (body).*
- *This craving does not surprise me.*
- *I knew it was coming.*
- *This is no big deal.*
- *It will pass.*
- *I am not going to let this craving control me.*
- *I will focus on the love of God my Father.*

Focusing on the love of God as your Father removes a law-based approach of trying to fight and overcome the addiction through willpower and self-effort. It removes you from being consumed by the craving. By trying to fight the addiction through willpower and self-effort, you eventually give in to the craving, surrendering to its urges. You have experienced this many times in your life.

A law-based approach to overcoming an addiction is telling yourself, "I Shall Not _____." Whatever addiction you fill in the blank with now preoccupies your thoughts. You try with your own effort to not do that behavior. But you fail.

This is how you have approached your addiction your entire life. This how the person in Romans 7:7-8:17 approached trying not to sin. He told himself, "I shall not covet." But the harder he tried not to covet, the more he coveted. This led him to discover the grace of God freely give to him in Jesus and the Spirit-filled life, which produced peace in his mind and brought him into a love relationship with God as "Abba, Father."

He learned in the Spirit-filled life it is through a loving relationship with God as Father that a person is able to put to death the sinful deeds of the body. He learned it is not through willpower and self-effort, a you-shall-not-covet, law-based approach to overcoming sin, but a grace-based approach where a person focuses on a loving relationship with God as Father.

This is what Paul was saying in Galatians 5:16 when he wrote, "*So I say, walk by the Spirit, and you will not gratify the desires of the flesh.*" To walk by the Spirit is to focus on God as your loving Father (Galatians 4:4-6). As long as a person takes a law-based, thou-shall-not-based approach, he will give in to the cravings of the flesh. But when he takes a grace-based approach by saying, "I am my Father's loved son," he will find peace.

5. Think about those you love and who love you. Get their pictures out.

6. Exercise

7. Visit someone who is a healthy person to be around.

8. Find something good to do for someone.

9. Read favorite passages, chapters, or books from the Bible.

10. Keep your vision for your life fresh in your mind and make decisions that help fulfill your vision.

11. Fast forward the consequences of giving into your cravings. Think about the pain and heartache giving in will cause in your life and in the lives of your loved ones.

12. Think about and list on paper the benefits of making the right decision.

Create Success Responses
Success responses are prepared responses to situations that trigger cravings. By thinking through specific scenarios you will face, tempting you to go back into your addiction, and preparing successful responses to them, you will not be taken by surprise when they come but will be ready to make the right decision and go the right direction.

Here are three examples of creating success responses when cravings come.

TEMPTING SITUATION - When I get angry with someone, such as my spouse or a person at work.

SUCCESSFUL RESPONSE – I will tell myself, "I am God my Father's loved son/daughter." Instead of depending on the addiction to calm me down, I will give grace to the person with whom I am angry because God has given grace to me.

TEMPTING SITUATION - I see someone from my past in the store and he asks me to come over to his house or go to a party.

SUCCESSFUL RESPONSE - I will tell myself, "I am God my Father's loved son/daughter." I will tell him I am in recovery and no longer live that lifestyle. If this person is truly my friend, he will respect my decision and be happy for me. If this person continues to try to get me to come with him, it will be a clear indication this person does not truly care for me.

TEMPTING SITUATION - I am home alone and a craving kicks in.

SUCCESSFUL RESPONSE – I will tell myself, "I am God my Father's loved son/daughter." I will call my sponsor immediately and pop the rubber band on my wrist.

Creating prepared responses to situations will help you tremendously as you respond to tempting situations. Think through all the situations that trigger cravings. Write them down. Then write down how you will respond in each situation.

Establish Boundaries
There are certain people you can't be around and specific places you cannot go. Set boundaries for yourself that will help you stay away from these people and places. Hold fast to your boundaries.

Give Your Friends And Family Time To Trust You
Don't Take Loss Of Trust Personally
Because of years of hiding, lying, and denying, your family and friends do not trust you. Don't take their lack of trust personally or live in self-condemnation because of it. Their lack of

trust doesn't mean they do not love you or have not forgiven you. They do love you and have forgiven you. Love and forgiveness is free. However, trust must be earned.

Just as trust is lost over time, it can be won back over time From this day forward, concentrate on winning back their trust by living an honest, open, and transparent life. It is very important to know that it may take years to earn back their trust. As you make progress, know you may never win back one-hundred percent trust, but you can win back much trust. And much trust is better than no trust.

I Will Get Mad If My Wife Doesn't Trust Me

Carl was a day away from graduating from the recovery program where I was a counselor and teacher. As he and I were making final preparations for his departure, he said if his wife hid her purse when he returned home, he would be mad at her.

I asked him why she might hide her purse. He said because he had stolen money, credit cards, and checks from her, as well as taken her keys during his addiction. I explained to him that he created the lack of trust she had for him and only he, by consistently making good decisions for the next months and years, could re-establish her trust.

He had no basis for getting mad at his wife should she hide her purse. She was only doing what he trained her to do in his years of hiding, lying, and denying. I encouraged him to go home and apologize to his wife for behaving in a way that forced her not be able to trust him. I also encouraged him to ask her forgiveness and tell her that if she needed to hide her purse, he totally understood, and one day he hoped to earn her trust back so she could be free in her own home to leave her purse out in the open.

Here are eight ways to earn back trust.

- Don't expect your family to immediately trust you.

- Don't defend yourself or get angry when they do not trust you or when they ask you questions.

- Give your family as much time as they need to trust you.

- Go where you said you were going, and be home when you said you would be home.

- Call them if you are going to be late.

- Answer your phone when they call.

- Give your family many reasons to trust you.

- Remember, losing trust happens immediately with one bad decision. Gaining trust happens eventually with many good decisions.

Don't Expect A Prodigal's Welcome Home Party
When the prodigal son returned home, his father threw him a joyful welcome home party. Most prodigals, when they return home from recovery, don't receive a welcome home party.

Remember, while you were in your addiction and in recovery, members of your family carried the weight of the problems at home. They may still be carrying bitterness toward you because of the history of your addiction. Give them grace and time to work through their own hurts and pain caused by the addiction. Give yourself grace, too.

As you awaken to the pain your addiction has caused in the lives of those you love, don't be hard on yourself. Forgive yourself and move forward, determined not bring any more pain into their lives or your own. Commit to bring only joy and happiness.

Spend The Rest Of Your Life Doing Good
You have spent enough time in your life doing things that have hurt yourself and others. Now, spend the rest of your life doing good things that will help yourself and others.

The Bible says that Jesus went around doing good (Acts 10:38). It also says to never tire of doing good (2 Thessalonians 3:13) and to never become weary or give up in doing good (Galatians 6:9). The Bible says if you continue to plant seeds of good, then one day you will reap a harvest of good from the good seeds you planted (Galatians 6:9).

No Exception, No Excuses, No Compromises
There will be times when you will be tempted to return to your addiction by allowing an exception to occur, making an excuse, or compromising. You will find yourself saying just this one time will not hurt, it will be okay, no one will know. But deep down you know there is no such thing as just one time. You know it will hurt yourself and others, and it is not okay. Avoid the just-one-time-will-not-hurt exception, excuse, and compromise...reject it immediately! Let no exceptions occur. Make no excuses. Have no compromises. A compromise today leads to a catastrophe tomorrow!

Do Not Escape The Pain, Endure The Pain
Life is hard...painful...difficult. It will have its problems and troubles. When these hardships come, do not seek to escape them through your addiction. Rather, persevere through them.

Better days will come if you persevere through the problems and pain of life. Numbing the pain through your addiction will only make your life more miserable.

Jesus said *"In this world you will have trouble, but take heart, I have overcome the world"* (John 16:33). With Jesus, you can overcome the trouble this world brings. So rather than escaping the troubles of the world through your addiction, know troubles will come, and when they do, trust Jesus.

Learning to trust God in the troubles of life will help you tremendously. Proverbs 3:5-6 encourages us with these words:

> *Trust in the LORD with all your heart, and lean not on your own understanding; In all your ways acknowledge Him, and He shall direct your paths.*

You may not always understand why things happen the way they do. You may have questions for God, and he's okay with your questions. But through it all, and no matter how you may feel, keep trusting him. He loves you!

Know God Is With You And Loves You
As you leave behind the bondage of your old life and move forward into a new life, know God is with you and he loves you. No matter how great your failures, God will never fail to love you. Let each morning bring you word of his unfailing love (Psalm 143:8).

Keep Your Vision Of A New Life Before You
Keep your vision always before you. Never lose sight of it. Your vision of a new life for yourself and your family will spur you on to make the right decisions.

Seek Professional Help If Needed
It may become necessary for you to seek professional help. There are people trained to help those who struggle with addictions. Find those who specialize in helping people break free from addictions. More than likely, your community has an outpatient or inpatient program available. If you choose a Christian recovery program, please know that some of them are legalistic in nature and do not teach the fullness of God's grace. However, God still works through these programs.

If you choose to go into a Christian program, take with you a few grace-based books. Take this book or other books I have written. I also recommend Bob George's, Andrew Farley's, Matt McMillen's, and Bob Christopher's books. Bob George's book, *Jesus Changes Everything* is one of the best books I have read. So I definitely recommend it!

Consider A Three-Month Program

Many inpatient programs are three months or longer. I highly recommend, at the very least, checking into a three-month program. I know that may seem like a long time, but compared to the rest of your life, three months is a short time. Three months are going to pass no matter what. It would be better for you to invest in your future by committing to a three month or longer recovery program than to allow three months to pass and your addiction become worse, or you even die.

The Spiritual High Will Fade Away

I have seen many people come out of treatment programs excited about their futures. Many coming out of Christian programs are on a spiritual high. They had a spiritual mountain-top experience while in recovery. And there is nothing wrong with that.

However, because they are on a spiritual high, they believe they are set free from their addiction and will never go back. Sadly, though, within days, weeks, or months, when the spiritual high wears off and real life sets in, many return to their addiction, even though they wholeheartedly believed they never would.

Please be aware, no matter how excited you are about Jesus, no matter how full of grace you are, you will still battle the flesh (Galatians 5:17) ...you still live in the world...and you still have an enemy in Satan who is committed to your destruction.

The flesh in the world is like a kid in a candy shop. Just like a candy shop offers a kid exciting, pleasurable temptations, the world offers the flesh these same pleasurable and exciting temptations. In recovery, the sinful cravings of the flesh sometimes lie dormant, giving the person graduating from recovery a false sense of security. But when he returns into the world, the flesh eventually surfaces with temptations to eat from the world's "candy shop." Don't be surprised when this happens, be prepared.

The spiritual high will soon fade away. Real life will soon set in. Problems will soon arise. Those old friends will soon start calling. Temptations will soon come. Cravings will eventually return. Don't think just because you had a spiritual experience the addiction is gone. The flesh doesn't care. The world doesn't care. Satan doesn't care. All will attack you. Once you leave the program, you will need a recovery plan to follow. Commitment to your plan is vital. By diligently working your plan daily, you will see amazing results and reap the abundance of rewards.

19

CONCLUSION

YOU HAVE SPENT MANY days and nights in hopelessness. You have wondered if you will ever be free from your addiction. You have wondered if your life will ever get better or if you will live in the misery of your addiction for the rest of your life. Silently, you have believed you will be in bondage to your addiction for the rest of your life.

I have good news for you...there is hope! The Bible says:

> I remember my affliction and my wandering, the bitterness and the gall. I well remember them, and my soul is downcast within me. Yet this I call to mind and therefore I have hope: Because of the Lord's great love we are not consumed, for his compassions never fail. They are new every morning; great is your faithfulness (Lamentation 3:19-23).

God's Grace Is Your Hope

The source of your hope is God's great love for you and his compassion and faithfulness to you. God's love, compassion, and faithfulness is his grace. God will never stop loving you. He is always there for you. He is committed to you through the good days and bad, through the ups and downs.

Every morning you wake up to the God who loves you more than you will ever know, who is full of compassion toward you, and who will never leave you.

Because of God's great love, compassion, and faithfulness, you have hope. With God, you can break free from your addiction. You can live beyond your addiction. You can experience a new life.

A New Life Is For You!

You may be tempted to believe experiencing new life is possible for other people but not for you. It is possible for you too!

God's grace is freely offered to all people. Revelation 22:17 says:

> *The Spirit and the bride say, "Come!" And let the one who hears say, "Come!" Let the one who is thirsty come; and let the one who wishes take the free gift of the water of life.*

The Spirit is the Spirit of Jesus saying to come take the free gift of the water of life...come drink of grace. The bride is all those who have already come and taken of the free gift of the water of life, who drank of grace. Together, Jesus and his bride are saying for you to come and drink of his grace. Grace is for all. Grace is for you.

Are you thirsty? Has your addiction left you parched? Is your heart dry? Come drink of grace.

Jesus, in his final meal with his disciples before his crucifixion, invited them to eat and drink of the new covenant of grace. You are invited by Jesus, too, the great giver of grace, to come and eat and drink of his grace. Come sit at the table of grace with all the others who are in need. Those who are hurting, those who are living in guilt, shame, and condemnation, come sit with them at the table of grace and experience the healing power of God's grace freely given to everyone in Jesus.

As you eat and drink of God's grace, you will begin to be restored. You will begin to be healed. You will begin to experience a new life.

Addicted To Grace Recovery Groups All Over The World!
My Vision For The Future

My vision for the future is to see *Addicted To Grace Recovery Groups* started all over the world. I envision *Addicted To Grace Recovery Conferences* you can bring your friends and family to, so they can also experience God's grace.

Through these groups and conferences, I envision healing happening for those living in the hopelessness of addiction. I see those once living in guilt now living in grace. I see people being set free and being used by God to set others free. I see people all over the world becoming addicted to grace and being ambassadors of grace in their communities. I would be delighted to come to your church and present the *Addicted To Grace Conference.*

Start Your Own Addicted To Grace Group

If God stirs your heart to do so, start your own *Addicted To Grace Recovery Group* in your community or church. You can use this book for your group meetings. I know you may feel inadequate to start a group. I know how you feel. I have battled feelings of inadequacy for most of my life. But that is what grace is about. That is what faith is about. By grace, through faith, start a group and see what God does through you!

Starting an *Addicted To Grace Recovery Group* may not be for everyone. God will use people in many other ways to share his grace. But I do know what God's desire is for everyone...he wants everyone to become addicted to grace!

I want to encourage you with the words from Revelation 22:21 as you embark on your journey of grace. Revelation 22:21, the very last verse in the Bible, says, *"The grace of the Lord Jesus be with God's people. Amen."*

On your best days his grace will be with you. On your worst days his grace will be with you. There will never be a time when his grace will not be with you. His grace will always be with you.

God loves you and wants a relationship with you. If you would like to begin a relationship with God, you can do so by placing your faith in Jesus. If this is your heart, below is a simple prayer to express your faith in Jesus.

God, I realize I was created to be in a relationship with you. Through grace, you have made it possible for me to be in this relationship. I admit I have sinned. However, because of your great love and kindness, Jesus came to earth to pay my sin penalty through his blood. He died for all of my sins. Because all of my sins were counted against Jesus in his death, you are no longer counting my sins against me. By faith, I accept your forgiveness. I believe Jesus arose from the dead. Today, I place my faith in Jesus. I am fully forgiven and totally accepted by you, in a relationship with you, and a person within who Jesus now lives.

If you made a decision to place your faith in Jesus, I celebrate with you. All of heaven celebrates with you. Welcome to God's family of grace.

ABOUT THE AUTHOR

In 1991, the story of God's grace intersected with the story of Brad's life when he read a book by Bob George called *Classic Christianity*. Since this time, his passion has been to share the life-changing truths of God's grace with as many people as possible in as many ways as possible. Some of the ways Brad shares the good news of God's grace is through writing, social media, speaking, and through his podcast. You can access his podcast on iTunes, Spotify, Google Podcasts, and other podcast hosts.

In addition to *Addicted To Grace*, Brad has written *The Story of Grace*. This book was written to help people understand the unfolding of God's grace to the human race through the person of Jesus and to experience God's grace in their lives.

He has also written *Strategic Church* and a booklet called *Paul and James: Were They Really In Agreement?* All of his writings are available on his website and Amazon. Brad's website is www.gracereach.info.

In addition to his books, Brad has many other resources on his website to help you grow in grace. There you will find his video teachings and many blogs he has written, as well as links to other grace teachers. You may also visit his YouTube channel and Facebook page.

For 13 years, Brad served as founder and Senior Pastor of Grace Church Gulf Coast. Prior to this, he attended Dallas Theological Seminary where he received a Master of Arts Degree in Christian Education. In addition, he served on staff with Campus Crusade for Christ for two years. He holds a Bachelor of Science Degree in Coaching and Sports Administration from the University of Southern Mississippi. He is married to Becky. Together they have three sons, Kyle, Philip, and Mark.

If you would like to contact Brad about speaking at your church, conference, retreat, or event, email him at bradr1966@gmail.com.

Made in the USA
Coppell, TX
28 March 2021